LEADERS OPEN DOORS

Leaders Open Doors

A Radically Simple Leadership Approach to Lift People, Profits, and Performance

BILL TREASURER

iUniverse, Inc.
Bloomington

LEADERS OPEN DOORS
A RADICALLY SIMPLE LEADERSHIP APPROACH TO
LIFT PEOPLE, PROFITS, AND PERFORMANCE

iUniverse books may be ordered through booksellers or by contacting:

iUniverse
1663 Liberty Drive
Bloomington, IN 47403
www.iuniverse.com
1-800-Authors (1-800-288-4677)

Because of the dynamic nature of the Internet, any web addresses or links contained in this book may have changed since publication and may no longer be valid. The views expressed in this work are solely those of the author and do not necessarily reflect the views of the publisher, and the publisher hereby disclaims any responsibility for them.

Any people depicted in stock imagery provided by Thinkstock are models, and such images are being used for illustrative purposes only.

Certain stock imagery © Thinkstock.

ISBN: 978-1-4759-7636-6 (sc)
ISBN: 978-1-4759-7638-0 (hc)
ISBN: 978-1-4759-7637-3 (e)

Library of Congress Control Number: 2013903616

Printed in the United States of America

iUniverse rev. date: 3/6/2013

Leaders Open Doors *is an amazing book! With a gazillion leadership books available, Bill Treasurer brings a powerful, practical treatment that uniquely reframes a quality still in short supply. Written with refreshing clarity, delightful humor, and profound insight, the book is a must-read for all interested in successfully influencing others to deliver their best.*

Chip R. Bell, author of *Managers as Mentors*

Yes, you can teach old dogs new tricks! If you think you've had your fill of leadership tomes, tricks, and tools ... don't walk away. Bill's wonderful ability to use word pictures and genuine and realistic examples makes this a wonderful treat ... one that teaches anyone, anywhere!

Beverly Kaye, founder and co-CEO,
Career Systems International
coauthor of *Help Them Grow or Watch Them Go: Career Conversations Employees Want*

Are you an open-door leader? The concept is simple but powerful. Read this book to find out how you can open doors and create more opportunities for yourself as a leader, those you lead, and your organization.

Mark Sanborn, president, Sanborn & Associates
author of *The Fred Factor*

In a simple yet powerful way, **Leaders Open Doors** *practices what it teaches! It opens the door to what makes leaders effective and leaves the reader with an array of practical suggestions to improve one's own capability as a leader. Kudos to Bill for getting to the heart of the matter in a way we can all use to become better leaders.*

Tony Scotto, EVP and chief development officer, ACI Worldwide, Inc.

To all the open-door leaders who helped me believe in myself, especially Henry L. Thompson, Bob Carr, Hines Brannan, Ft. Vince Malatesta, and O. K. Sheffield.

One hundred percent of the author's royalties from the sales of this book are being donated to organizations that provide opportunities for people with special needs.

Contents

Preface

My five-year-old son, Ian, is a preschooler at the Asheville Montessori School in Asheville, North Carolina, where we live. Each Monday his teachers pick one person to be the "class leader" for the day. I only became aware of this because one sunny afternoon Ian came bounding up the stairs proclaiming, "Guess what, Daddy—I got to be the class leader today!"

Being the class leader would be a big deal for any five-year-old kid. For Ian, who is used to playing second fiddle to his more dominant firstborn twin brother and sister, Alex and Bina, being selected as the first fiddle was even more special. Ian's exuberance caught my attention.

"Really? Class leader? That's a big deal, little buddy. What did you get to do as the class leader?"

Ian's answer was simple, funny, and in its own way, profound.

"I got to open doors for people!"

In a matter of fifteen seconds, with seven simple words, Ian clarified what's most important about leadership.

How Leaders Serve Up Opportunities

I'm one of those people who can get all knotted up by overthinking simple ideas. I love it when wise people like my five-year-old son can cut straight to what matters most. Ian is right: to be a leader is to open doors for others. Leaders open doors of perception, possibility, and, most importantly, opportunity. *This book is about how leaders help people and organizations by creating opportunities for growth.* It is about the responsibility that leaders have for noticing, identifying, and mostly creating opportunities for the benefit of people, organizations, and society. I call it open-door leadership.

WE COMPLEXIFY LEADERSHIP

In his role as class leader, Ian quickly learned an essential lesson about leadership. Opening doors is pretty much what matters most about leading people. Yet many adults make the topic of leadership far more complex and overwhelming. Leadership is the most overanalyzed, thoroughly dissected, and utterly confused topic in business. In addition to umpteen thousands of books on the subject, there are leadership blogs, seminars, webinars, and retreats, all peddled by leadership gurus and consultants. I know. I am one of them.

For over half of my life, I have studied leadership. I began because in one of my earlier jobs I discovered that I was a lousy leader. One of my employees told me so ... after threatening to quit because of my dictatorial behavior. More on that later.

After discovering how pathetically bad I was as a leader, I started reading books on leadership and management. I got better as a leader. As a result, I decided to go to graduate school and did my thesis on leadership.

And that's when it started. That's when I became an official contributor to the complexification of leadership. My thesis assessed—take a deep breath—*the efficacy of the initiation of psychological structure through the use of directive leadership styles as a negative correlate of role ambiguity and positive correlate of employee satisfaction in workplaces that have undergone a recent reduction in force.*

Since graduate school two decades ago, my contributions

to the complexification of leadership have only gotten more pronounced. I worked for two small leadership and team-building companies. Later, I was an executive in the change management and human performance practice at Accenture, one of the world's largest consulting firms. I eventually became the company's first full-time internal executive coach. Building on those experiences, in 2002 I founded my own management consulting company (Giant Leap Consulting) and have since designed, developed, and delivered leadership workshops for thousands of employees in prominent organizations throughout the world. I've authored a comprehensive off-the-shelf leadership-facilitator training program and two not-so-simple books.

I have become a senior officer in the legion of consultants who make their livelihood by plumbing, parsing, and peddling leadership. I can complexify with the best of them. The more my consulting compatriots and I complexify leadership by using fancy-pants words and nitpicking the life out of the subject, the more we can charge you for our specialized leadership hocus-pocus. Sure, most of us are well intentioned, but by overanalyzing the subject, we've muddled up the concept of leadership.

We leadership experts, sadly, have made it harder for people to be leaders. As the checklist for what it takes to be a leader gets longer, more idealized, and more complicated, the expectations that we hold leaders to keep shifting, causing people to opt out of the chance to lead. The standards of what it means to be a leader have been raised beyond people's reach. The expectations that leaders are held to have become so inflated that practically no one can categorically qualify as a "leader" anymore. We expect leaders to be bold *and* calculated, passionate *and* reasonable, rational *and* emotional, confident *and* humble, driven *and* patient, strategic *and* tactical, competitive *and* cooperative, principled *and* flexible. Of course, it *is* possible to be all of those things … if you're God!

I Resign from the Legion of Leadership Complexifiers (LLC)

This book represents my full resignation from the ranks of the Legion of Leadership Complexifiers. I pledge to you that I will speak plainly and simply. Too many books, including my earlier ones, are too dense and bloated with big SAT words, fancy quadrant models, and research citations from obscure academic journals. It's all part of the complexification business. But after a quarter of a century as a ranking member of the LLC, this complexification stuff bores and exhausts me. The density weighs me down. I suspect it weighs you down too. Reading a book shouldn't exhaust you like a long day at work.

My resignation is driven by a few changes in my own life. First, I'm older and, frankly, less insecure. When I was in my twenties, thirties, and forties, proving how smart I was took up too much of my time. Now that I'm in my fifties, I am more interested in having ideas connect with you than in validating my intellect.

Second, having led hundreds of client engagements throughout my career and having spoken to thousands of people across the world, I've come to know that the ideas that get through to people are those that are easiest to understand. Simple ideas are those that are self-evident and effective. More importantly, simple ideas are those that get used.

The third change driving my resignation from the leadership-complexification ranks is that I'm the father of three children. They have taught me that we career-minded grown-ups are often just too smart for our own good, which is dumb. We're better off thinking about leadership with the clarity and simplicity of a five-year-old child. When I want my kids to get something done, like a house chore, I don't talk about the *strategic value-added proposition of goal attainment*; I talk about the opportunity they'll create by getting the work done. *Yes*, kids, you *can* have ice cream … right after you clean up your room. Simple, not complex!

We Can Simplify Leadership

Faced with an ever-longer and ever-changing list of leadership criteria, who could possibly be successful as a leader, much less want to be one? Maybe it's time to lighten the leadership load a little. Maybe it's time to get back to the basic idea that leaders are simply creators of opportunity for others: they open doors. I wrote this book to bring leadership back to that simple idea.

Open-door leadership is a simple concept that you can quickly grasp and enjoy putting into practice. My hope is that the concepts make it appealing for you to opt *in* to the chance to lead. If you are in a position to open doors for people by creating opportunities that help them grow, you are a leader. This book will be especially useful if you are

- new to the leadership ranks,
- a seasoned executive but feeling uninspired in your leadership role,
- frustrated by the apathy and lack of motivation shown by your direct reports,
- at the "give back" stage in your career where helping others succeed is especially gratifying,
- confused about the topic of leadership (maybe because of the glut of bloated leadership books!), or
- wanting to be a better and more effective leader.

The aim of this book is simple: to inspire you to open doors of opportunity for the people you lead.

How This Book Opens Doors for You

As you read this book, you will be introduced to six unique doors of opportunity. The book is divided into two sections. The first section, "Before the Door," presents the first three chapters and will ground you in the book's foundational concepts. The second section, "Doors of Opportunity," covers six chapters, each describing a unique opportunity door. This book is meant to be a fast and useful read. It is also designed to help you take immediate action. So at the conclusion of each chapter, you'll be provided with some specific actions and reflection questions to provide momentum toward strengthening your open-door leadership.

Chapter and page number	What you'll understand	Key chapter takeaways
Preface: Page xi	what a leader is, simply	☐ Leadership should be simple, not complex. ☐ A leader creates opportunities for others.
Chapter 1: Page 3 "Introducing Open-Door Leadership"	why leadership means opening doors	☐ Open-door leaders have four skills: knowing their employees, matching suitedness, envisioning the desired results, and providing ongoing support.
Chapter 2: Page 11 "Opportunity Focus"	why focusing on problem solving is far less effective than focusing on the opportunities those "problems" nearly always provide	☐ Leaders fill people with courage. ☐ Pull through opportunity; don't push through fear. ☐ Sharpen your own opportunity focus.

A Word before You Start

The approach to leadership described in this book is based on the simple and well-tested idea that leaders help people and organizations grow when they focus on creating opportunities for others. But just because the idea is simple doesn't mean it is easy. Open-door leadership takes work. So let's get started. How do you start opening doors for people, and what's in it for you if you do? Turn to the first section to find out.

SECTION 1

BEFORE THE DOOR

Being an open-door leader requires having an understanding of what an open-door leader does. It also means having an opportunity mind-set, a significant shift from the more common threat-focused way of leading. Many leaders hyperfocus on mitigating risk, viewing most situations as threats and problems. But when leaders view situations as risks, threats, and problems, they inject fear and anxiety into people, generating pessimism. In the long run, fear damages both morale and performance.

Open-door leaders view challenging situations as opportunities, not problems. Instead of injecting people with fear, they help people see the opportunities that challenges provide, inspiring them with excitement and hope. The resulting optimism lifts morale and performance.

In this section you'll discover

- the four skills of an open-door leader,
- why your approach to opportunity matters,
- why using fear to motivate people makes for lousy leadership, and
- why making people uncomfortable is one of an open-door leader's most important jobs.

CHAPTER 1

Introducing Open-Door Leadership

All that is valuable in human society depends upon the opportunity for development accorded the individual.
—Albert Einstein

Leadership is often defined as a set of behaviors by which one person influences others toward the achievement of goals. Put more simply, leadership is about momentum and results. While these definitions are true, they somehow fall short. What mechanism should a leader use, for example, to "influence" strong performance? Has leadership evolved beyond carrots and sticks? And what about the people being led? Besides a paycheck, what do they get out of getting results for the leader? What's in it for them? After all, the leader's success depends on them, right?

What's missing is *opportunity*. In exchange for advancing the leader's goals, the people being led should expect work opportunities that provide for

- growth and personal development,
- career fulfillment and enrichment,
- acquisition of new skills,
- financial gain and other rewards, and
- greater access to leadership roles.

People and organizations grow and develop to the extent that they capitalize on opportunities to do so. Opportunities are important to leaders because they're important to the people they lead. Opportunities are the venues where people can try themselves, test themselves, better themselves, and even find themselves. The leader's job is to match the opportunity to the person and to help the person, and the organization, exploit the opportunity for all it's worth. Open-door leadership is about noticing, identifying, and creating opportunities for those being led.

Think for a moment about a leader whom you greatly admire. Pick someone who has led you rather than someone on the world stage. What do you admire about him or her? Did he open a door to an opportunity where you could grow your skills or improve yourself, such as asking you to lead a high-profile project? Did she help illuminate a blind spot by giving you candid feedback that caused you to see yourself in a different and more honest way? Did he build your confidence by asking for your perspective, input, and ideas? Or did she openly advocate for your promotion, showing you how much she valued you? What doors did he open for you?

My bet is that the leaders you most admire are the ones who left you better off than they found you by creating opportunities that helped you grow. How?

- by being open *to* you, valuing your input and perspective
- by being open *with* you, telling you the truth even if the truth is difficult to hear
- by helping you be receptive to new possibilities and experiences and new ways of perceiving and thinking

Open-door leadership involves creating or assigning opportunities in order to promote growth. By promoting the growth of those they lead, leaders increase the likelihood of their own success and advancement. They also increase the likelihood of creating other leaders, which is essential to building a lasting leadership legacy. Leaders create leaders by opening doors of opportunity that have a positive and lasting impact on the behavior of those they lead.

"Open Door" Is Not a Policy!

To be clear, open-door leadership is not about having an open-door *policy*. Such policies are just more management hokum. One of the surest signs of a rookie leader is the claim "I have an open-door policy, and my door is always open so my employees can get to me." If ever there were a recipe for lousy leadership, it is to allow yourself to be continuously interrupted by people. If your door is always open, how on earth would you effectively get any work done on behalf of the people who interrupt you? Open-door leadership is *not* about having a policy of keeping your door open *to* others. It *is* about taking actions to open doors *for* others. It is about so much more than giving people unfettered access to you.

I Knew an Open-Door Leader

After having spoken with thousands of executives over the course of two decades, I am convinced that career advancement is nearly always a function of the presence, influence, and support of a dedicated open-door leader. They always seem to appear when we need them, nudging us along, encouraging our growth, and helping us see and move toward our potential.

Let me share a very personal story about one such leader's profound impact on my life and career. The story helps illustrates the concept of open-door leadership and introduces four skills that open-door leaders possess.

I used to drink too much. Way too much. I drank to the point where my drinking started interfering with my life and relationships. Then I entered a recovery program and got help. Life got better.

Three years after getting sober and attending lots of support-group meetings, I decided to reveal to my boss, a partner at Accenture, that I was in recovery. After working for him for three years, I wanted him to know me beyond the person he knew me to be at work.

Keep in mind that Accenture is not some young, urban start-up company with a foosball table in the break room. It is one of the world's largest management and technology consulting firms. The culture is, at once, professional, disciplined, ambitious, and ... stiff. Though I didn't expect my boss to pat me on my shoulder and say, "Good for you; you're a drunk!" I expected more of a reaction than I got. After I told him that I was in recovery, my boss looked at me quizzically, and muttered, "I see." Then he made some small-talk comments and hurried on to another meeting.

I regretted having told him and wondered whether I had just damaged my career.

Then, about two weeks later, he called me into his office and said, "I've been thinking about what you told me a few weeks ago. What I didn't tell you then is that I am the chairman of the board of directors of a nonprofit agency called the Georgia Council on Substance Abuse. It's based here in Atlanta. Accenture recently agreed to do a pro bono research project, and we're going to be providing them with a small team to do the research. I'd like for you to lead the project. Remember, I'm the board chair, so I'm going to be here with you every step of the way."

Door open.

My boss had created an opportunity for me to align my career goals and my personal interests with Accenture's goals in serving the client.

It was the first time as a new manager that I got to lead my own project team. Given my personal experience with substance abuse, you can imagine how high my passion was for the work. With that passion, and the support of my boss, I did a great job. Because I did a great job, new doors opened and I got other meaningful projects.

There are a number of factors at play in this story.

1. First, to open a door for me, my boss had to have a fuller knowledge of my background than just my current skills. He had to know what I wanted to achieve with my career and the contribution I was hoping to make. He also had to know something about my outside-of-work identity.
2. Second, he had to make the connection between an opportunity that existed and my *suitedness* to take advantage of it.
3. Third, he had to have a clear picture about how the opportunity could benefit the company and me. The opportunity would need to deepen my experience and increase my skills, making me a more valuable employee for the company.
4. Fourth, he had to have a genuine interest in seeing me succeed. In short, he had to care about me.

Using this story as an example, we can draw out the four skills that open-door leaders commonly apply. They are:

*   **Knowing Your Employees:** Have extensive knowledge about the backgrounds, needs, and desires of your employees. Invest time in getting to know your employees beyond the tasks they get done for you. Ask them directly about their career goals and aspirations—what do *they* want to get out of this job? Keep in mind the goal isn't to intrude or interrogate. It's to gain insight into their goals, strengths, and motivations. There is more about this in the coming chapters.

- **Matching Suitedness:** Draw connections between the opportunity and the developmental needs of your employees. This involves constantly being on the lookout for opportunities that can boost the career advancement of your employees. Then, when opportunities are identified, ask, "Whose growth and development would pursuing this opportunity most advance?"

- **Envisioning the Desired Results:** Have a clear picture of the desired benefits that given opportunities present for the employees and the organization. Once an opportunity is assigned, do some "future-casting" with your employee, thinking through the potential benefits—to the employee and to the organization—that could emerge if the opportunity is successfully accomplished. Also give some thought to the actions that will have to occur to maximize the probability of success.

- **Providing Ongoing Support:** Genuinely want, and support, your employees' success. This skill is an outgrowth of the other three. When you really know the aims of your employees, when you've assigned them to a juicy opportunity that's ripe for their skills, and when you've worked with them to develop a clear picture of a successful outcome, you almost can't help but take a strong interest in their success. Still, stay involved by periodically asking what support they need from you, removing barriers that might block their progress, and offering encouragement and guidance when they meet with roadblocks and bottlenecks.

The more you cultivate these skills, the more you will see opportunities to open doors for others. The starting place is having a strong opportunity focus, the subject of the next chapter.

OPEN-DOOR ACTIONS AND REFLECTIONS:

- Think back over the course of your career. What are some opportunities that have been given to you? How have those opportunities helped you grow personally and professionally?

- Which opportunity stands out as particularly important? Who brought the opportunity to you? What is your impression of him or her as a leader? Why do you think you were selected for the opportunity instead of someone else?

- Look over the four skills of an open-door leader. Which ones did the person who brought you the opportunity use? Based on what you've read so far about open-door leadership, was the person who brought you the opportunity an open-door leader?

CHAPTER 2

Opportunity Focus

*Opportunity is more powerful even
than conquerors and prophets.*
—Benjamin Disraeli

Do you aim to be a problem-focused leader or an opportunity-focused leader?

Many work environments place a premium on leaders with critical-thinking and problem-solving skills. Often, though, that premium places too much emphasis on being *critical* and dealing with *problems*. In such workplaces, leaders can become downers, always harping on what's wrong and what needs to be fixed. Such leaders often resort to stoking people's fears to motivate them to get things done. This fear-stoking is exemplified by one of the most overused phrases in the history of business: *What keeps me awake at night ...*

Think about it. When leaders talk about (or more often *brag* about) what keeps them awake at night, aren't they really just showcasing their fears and anxieties? It's as if some leaders believe that the only way they'll get any rest is to make the entire workforce share in their fears. Unless people are as afraid as they are, they think that no one will be motivated enough to address whatever is causing the leaders to lose sleep. Seriously, putting people on the leader's twenty-four-hour fear cycle isn't motivating at all. Insomnia shouldn't be a leadership badge of honor.

Leaders would be better served to talk about what gets them up in the morning instead of what keeps them awake at night. Opportunity attracts and excites employees more than problems do. People want to follow leaders who have confidence in them and the opportunities that the future holds. People want to follow leaders who sleep soundly at night.

ARE YOU A SPILLER OR A FILLER?

Leaders generally fall into two broad categories: *spillers* and *fillers*. Spillers motivate people by stoking their fears. They view most situations as threats to be controlled and neutralized. When confronting a challenging situation, they immediately jump to the worst possible potential outcomes. By injecting you with fear and anxiety, they drain off your confidence and courage— hence the term "spiller." Always expecting a catastrophe, spillers blow things way out of proportion. They say things like,

- You have a huge problem on your hands.
- Do you realize how much that puts us at risk?
- If you mess up, we'll all be in trouble.
- Do not, I repeat, *do not* make a mistake.

Fillers, conversely, motivate people by appealing to their innate desire to excel. Instead of playing not to lose, as spillers do, fillers play to win. They look at the same situation but look for opportunities to exploit, not threats to control. Instead of transmitting fear and anxiety, they give followers a fuller sense of confidence and excitement. They say things like,

- Hmm, this is a challenging situation … and it's full of *opportunity*.
- Here's why I think you're the right person to take

on this challenge and why it would be good for your career growth.

- I have every confidence that you'll be successful, and here's the support you can expect from me ...
- What do *you* think? What should be our first steps?

Keep in mind that both fillers *and* spillers can get a good job out of you. For spillers, you may perform well because you know how much trouble you'll get into if you don't. For fillers, you'll perform well because they believe in you and you don't want to let them down.

But there is one consequential difference between working for a spiller and working for a filler. Fillers get deep loyalty from the people they lead. Spillers get deep resentments.

OPEN-DOOR LEADER EXAMPLES

Opportunities come in many forms. Sometimes they simply present themselves at an opportune moment. Other times they are intentionally created by the open-door leader. Here are some real-life examples:

- The owner of a respected construction company notices that one of the company's midlevel managers seems particularly skilled at building client relationships and winning work. At the same time, he is aware that there is no successor to the company's VP of business development, who is a few years away from retirement. He reassigns the manager to work directly with the VP with an eye toward his eventually becoming the VP's successor. The owner has the opportunity to fill a position with a qualified person, and the manager has the opportunity to grow into a position where he can excel.

- The managing director of a large consulting firm tasks a new manager with facilitating the director's weekly staff meeting while he's on a two-week overseas business trip. Every meeting attendee is more senior than the manager, including his former boss. The managing director knew that the manager was looking for more opportunities to demonstrate leadership and that facilitating a dominating group of senior execs would be a great start.
- The executive committee of a $300 million company decides to mobilize a small "Lessons Learned" team comprised of emerging leaders to conduct postmortems on large successful and unsuccessful projects. Each team member is assigned to the team based not on the skills that he or she currently has but on the skills that the organization needs them to grow. The team is responsible for gathering lessons and best practices and making recommendations to the executive committee.
- During the early parts of a three-day strategic-planning offsite meeting, the senior executive team of a medical device company receives a call from the home office confirming that the FDA is recommending a recall of one of the company's products. Instead of canceling the offsite, the execs decide that the emergency presents an opportunity for their successors—who are back in the home office—to lead the company through a substantial challenge. The execs make themselves available for morning and evening conference calls to stay apprised and lend support and direction.

WHY LEADING THROUGH FEAR IS CHEAP LEADERSHIP

If you're a parent, you know that using threats is an effective way of getting your children to do what you want them to do. Whether you're threatening to remove something your kids want or threatening to punish them for some naughty thing they're doing, fear works. I know. I've used it myself, even on my sweet five-year-old son, Ian. When he was going through his terrible twos and being disobedient, I would threaten to put on a Halloween mask that scared him to get him to be good. "Ian!" I'd bark. "Stop that right now or I'm going to put on the mask!" Though the Department of Social Services might not have approved of my scare tactics, they worked. All it took for me to quickly shift Ian from naughty to nice was the simple threat of a scary face.

Using fear to motivate people is cheap leadership. Any two-bit dictator can use fear to get things done. It takes no finesse or intelligence and ultimately works against the leader. The temporary spike in motivation from stoking people's fears is offset by the long-term impacts of deep resentment, performance-draining anxiety, and ill will. More evolved and thoughtful leaders choose to pull people toward the behaviors they want instead of pushing them from the behaviors they don't want. My wife, for example, uses a *compliment* system to promote good behavior with Ian, Alex, and Bina. Each time one of them finishes a chore, for example, they get to put a small stone (a "compliment") in a jar that's been set aside just for them. When they've gathered enough stones, they get a small reward, like dinner at Chuck E. Cheese.

If you want workers to act like adults, you have to lead like an adult. Instead of constantly drawing their attention to the bad things that will happen if they mess up, work with them to identify the actions and priorities that will increase their likelihood of succeeding. Remind them that taking on challenges is how leaders earn their merit badges at work. Be sure to also specify what rewards they can expect if they succeed—including the chance to be involved in more opportunities. Pulling people toward good behavior instead of threatening them out of bad behavior is a healthier and more mature way of leading.

Opportunity Attracts

Fear and excitement prompt the same neurological responses. Think for a moment about what happens to you, physiologically, when you are really, really afraid. Your heart races, your palms sweat, your breath gets faster and shorter, and your stomach teems with butterflies. Well, guess what? Those same physiological responses happen when you are going to have sex!

Fear and excitement are both high-arousal states. Though there are almost no neurological and physiological differences, there is one critical distinction between the conditions of fear and excitement. You experience fear as *displeasure,* and you experience excitement as *pleasure.* It follows that you move toward situations that provide pleasure and you avoid situations that provoke displeasure. By viewing and explaining situations as opportunities, you create a field of excitement where employees are more apt to face challenges than shirk them.

Focusing on opportunity instead of problems is not just a matter of semantics. Here are some specific impacts of keeping an opportunity focus:

- **Opportunity Pulls:** Leading by stoking people's fears provokes anxiety and negative thoughts of impending painful consequences. Opportunities are hopeful situations that evoke positive thoughts of pleasurable rewards. Leadership is most effective when it moves people toward a desired outcome rather than getting them to run away from a bad outcome. Opportunity attracts; fear repels.
- **Opportunity Points in the Right Direction:** When you are talking about opportunities, you are talking about the conditions you want instead of

the conditions you want to prevent from happening. Because outcomes often follow the direction of our thoughts, it's best to focus on what you want vs. what you don't. "Our opportunity is to keep the ball in the air" is better than "Whatever you do, don't drop that ball!"

- **Opportunity Activates Imagination**: We "take advantage of" or "capitalize on" opportunities. They are conditions that don't yet exist and require people's hard work and imagination to be fully exploited.
- **Opportunity Inspires Courage:** Opportunities are not "sure things." The positive outcome you hope to create is not guaranteed. Thus opportunities come with potential risks. The risk is what infuses the pursuit of opportunities with pleasurable excitement.
- **Opportunity Begets Opportunity:** Wouldn't you rather have your employees coming to you with new ideas and opportunities they want you to *support* instead of problems they want you to *resolve?* When you model opportunistic thinking, you increase the likelihood of building a self-sufficient, "can do" spirit among employees.

OF BIG OS AND LITTLE OS

Capitalizing on a really big opportunity often requires marshaling a host of smaller opportunities across an organization. In these instances, the open-door leader's job is to broaden the opportunity landscape for the entire organization. To illustrate this concept, consider the story of Sutton Bacon. To the surprise of many, Sutton became the president and CEO of the Nantahala Outdoor Center (NOC) in his late twenties. People wondered how a guy so young could be given the opportunity to lead a whitewater-adventure facility with such a rich history. But the choice made sense. Though young, Sutton was perfectly suited for the job. He had previously been the president of American Whitewater and, after graduating from Emory University in Atlanta, had worked as a marketing strategy consultant. What mattered more was how deeply Sutton loved the NOC. He had learned to kayak there when he was five years old. He knew, and valued, the NOC's rich history. He also knew of its financial struggles and competitive threats. A new year-round whitewater facility had just opened up in Charlotte, North Carolina, just two hours down the road. Sutton, part kayaker and part hard-core business consultant, convinced the NOC's board of directors that he was the right guy for the job.

For Sutton, the big opportunity was to create long-term sustainability for the NOC. That would require solidifying the NOC's preeminence as a whitewater mecca while expanding its offerings. The challenge for Sutton and his team was to get the bulk of the workforce—raft guides—to see that the NOC's opportunities would be limited if it continued thinking of itself as being a rafting business. Far more opportunities could be created for everyone by becoming an adventure business. More customers could be served, more money could be made, and more fun could be had if the NOC went beyond being a rafting outfitter to become a provider of memorable *adventure experiences*.

Becoming a world-leading provider of adventure experiences would require changing or reinvigorating nearly every aspect of the NOC. Sutton and his management team aimed at the larger opportunity (sustainability) by creating many smaller opportunities. They started hosting more national and international canoeing and kayaking competitions, which brought more exposure to the NOC and more revenues to fund other ideas. They launched more informal events too, like the annual Halloween Pumpkin Run, where kayakers competed by scooping up bobbing pumpkins on their way down through the rapids. They opened Slow Joe's Café, a small sandwich shop right at the river's edge. They even successfully convinced the leaders in Bryson City, North Carolina, to lift the NOC's alcohol license restrictions. People could now buy a beer and wine from the NOC instead of bringing it in their coolers.

The more opportunities Sutton and his team created, the more money they had to create more. They started an instant-photo business whereby families could purchase high-quality photos of themselves immediately after storming down the river. They opened an outdoor store in downtown Gatlinburg, Tennessee, and a LEED-certified retail store in the historic Grove Park Inn in Asheville, North Carolina.

Most importantly, Sutton and his team significantly increased the number and types of adventure programs available to customers. In addition to whitewater rafting and kayaking, programs now included things like ziplining, jet boat rides, mountain biking, high-ropes excursions, fly fishing, and international adventure excursions. The NOC was now squarely in the business of adventure.

Sutton and his team of open-door leaders had broadened the NOC's opportunity landscape. They were shifting people's thinking of the NOC from a North Carolina summertime rafting outfitter to a world-class commercial business enterprise offering unique adventure experiences. As a result of tightly marrying thrilling adventure *and* sound business, the NOC was becoming sustainable. Sutton even testified before the US House of Representatives Small Business Committee, where he was honored as by the committee as a "Hero of Small Business."

In the process of broadening the NOC's overall opportunity landscape, Sutton himself became an open-door leader. None of the opportunities his company expanded into could have been accomplished without Sutton opening the doors for his team to try new ideas and grow into new positions.

Bear in mind that the opportunities that Sutton and his team created weren't without hardship. Some of the NOC's most tenured personnel fiercely resisted the changes. They felt like the balance had swung too far toward capitalism and too far away from the commune culture they had worked so hard to create. A few people left. A few were asked to leave.

Opportunities bring about change, and change often comes with turbulence. Some people may find them threatening and disruptive and thus lag to embrace them. Open-door leaders have to be patient with the long game, giving people time to catch on to the potential that the opportunities hold.

The most satisfying opportunities are those that benefit customers *and* employees. It became important, for example, for Sutton and his team to make sure that the staff directly benefited from the changes. Sutton and his team lobbied for, and were granted, limited access to the Cheoah River, a scenic class IV and V river. Now the staff could paddle a remote and unspoiled river that had been closed off to kayakers for years. Next they created new play holes on the Nantahala River, which were irresistible fun for kayaking enthusiasts among the staff. Finally, they added Wi-Fi throughout the NOC outpost so staff and customers could access the Internet. People started to "get it." The best days of the NOC were in front of it, not behind it.

Eventually, all of the opportunities, big and small, helped transform the NOC and its culture. Many of the NOC's staff took pride in knowing that they had helped the NOC become the largest outdoor recreation company in the United States, offering more than 120 different adventure programs in ten states serving up to a million visitors annually. The *New York Times* recognized the NOC as the nation's premier paddling school, *Outside Magazine* called it the best place to learn how to paddle, and *National Geographic Adventure Magazine* declared it one of the best outfitters on earth.

OPEN-DOOR LEADERS ARE OPPORTUNITY CREATORS

A leader's primary job is to actively create opportunities that bring about real and concrete benefits. A leader should leave us better off than they found us. Open-door leaders don't sell hope. In fact they don't *sell* anything. They build. They experiment. They act. They create. And like Sutton and his team, by relentlessly focusing on creating opportunities for customers and employees, they open lots and lots of doors.

OPEN-DOOR ACTIONS AND REFLECTIONS:

* Write down your answers to these questions:
    1. What are some work-related opportunities or goals that "get you up in the morning"?
    2. In your work, what are you most excited about right now? Increase the time you spend doing things that awaken your spirit at work!
* Identify one work-related "problem" that is currently causing you anxiety. List the specific opportunities that this challenge presents. From now on, whenever you speak about this work challenge, refer to it as an *opportunity*.
* Identify one leader you've worked with and admire. Using the continuum below, place an *X* on the spot that best reflects the focus of the leader. Resist the temptation to say, "It depends on the situation." Just think in general terms.
* Now think of a leader with whom you've worked that you least admire. Use the same continuum to mark their spot.
* Now consider your focus. Where on the continuum is your predominant focus?

problem-focused   opportunity-focused

0   1   2   3   4   5   6   7   8   9   10

The leader you most admire likely has more of an opportunity focus than the leader you least admire. If you want to be admired too, you'll focus on raising your opportunity-focus number. Do that by reaching out to the admired leader for mentoring. Ask:

- When you come up against a challenging situation, what are your first thoughts?
- In your career, who influenced you to view challenges as opportunities?
- What advice can you give for helping me see the opportunities that challenging situations present?

CHAPTER 3

Purposeful Discomfort

*Move out of your comfort zone. You can only
grow if you are willing to feel awkward and
uncomfortable when you try something new.*
—Brian Tracy

As creators of opportunity, open-door leaders are providers of purposeful discomfort. Why? Ginny Rometty, the CEO of IBM, has it right when she says, "Growth and comfort do not coexist."[1] We grow, develop, and progress by pursuing opportunities that put us outside of our comfort zone. Opportunities create discomfort.

The trick is that you have to provide uncomfortable opportunities that provoke growth, not set people up for failure. As leader, you have to provide tasks or situations that are enough of a stretch that they motivate people to move outside of their comfort zones but not so far outside that they debilitate performance. While some level of fear and anxiety is natural, and perhaps even necessary, too much—see the previous chapter—is demoralizing and causes people to stew with resentment.

By nudging people into discomfort, you help activate their

---

1   Speaking at the *Fortune* Magazine Most Powerful Women Summit, October 5, 2011, http://youtu.be/Du_a0CCJkWE.

courage. Courage is what they need to face the fear that the discomfort provokes. Consider, for example, some of these common uncomfortable work situations and the opportunities they present for people to experience courage:

- giving a presentation to your boss's boss
- taking a job with demands that eclipse your current skills
- delegating a risky task to a new or untested employee
- enforcing new performance standards on employees who are longer tenured than you
- admitting to a client or customer that you or your company made a big mistake

It may surprise you that your job as an open-door leader is to make people uncomfortable, but good opportunities create discomfort. When you are asked to lead a group of employees for your very first time, that is an opportunity. It's also uncomfortable. When you are asked to make a new product pitch to the board of directors, that is an opportunity. It is also uncomfortable. When you are slotted to be your boss's successor, that is an opportunity. It's also uncomfortable. If something is uncomfortable, there's a good chance that it presents an opportunity to grow.

DELIVER DISCOMFORT IN DOSES

A large Chicago-based construction company uses purposeful discomfort as a key feature of its leadership-succession program. Each bimonthly leadership workshop starts by having each of the twenty-five up-and-coming leaders give a two-minute presentation. The focus is the progress they've made using the leadership concepts that they were introduced to during the previous workshops. Keep in mind that the presentations are videotaped and given in front of the company's most senior executives ... including the

CEO. Getting out of their comfort zones by giving two-minute presentations serves two purposes:

1. It holds them accountable to actually implementing the program concepts.
2. It forces them to deal with the discomfort that so often comes with giving a presentation.

When you watch the videotapes of the participants, you can see the arc of their progress. The confidence that these leaders gain in giving presentations during the course of the eighteen-month program is nothing short of amazing. Early on, most of the leaders are like awkward teenagers, stumbling through their two minutes, hemming and hawing and umming. Plenty of them suffer from an all-out brain freeze, stopping altogether, not knowing what to say next. But by the last workshop, everyone is able to stand and speak with confidence and poise. They've grown because they did something uncomfortable on purpose. As the program progresses, they become more comfortable with discomfort.

You have to be able to present confidently if people are to believe in the direction you set as their leader. So if you're in a leadership-development program with the aim of becoming a more confident and influential leader, you'd better learn how to present. That requires stepping straight into your *dis*comfort zone. And if you're leading the aspiring leaders, your job is to create the opportunity for them to experience their discomfort.

Create Safe Discomfort

Getting people to do purposefully uncomfortable things is easier if you also create safety for them. They have to know that you have their back, that the discomfort won't be permanent, and that it's truly purposeful. Otherwise, they'll think that you're a mad scientist and they're guinea pigs in some diabolical experiment. For example, before the high-potential leaders started regularly giving their two-minute presentations, the CEO explained how presenting was connected to the concept of leadership, that it was fully expected that they'd make lots of mistakes, and that they should seek progress, not perfection. The CEO, whom everyone admired for being a great communicator, also let people know that he started out as a terrible public speaker but forced himself to improve by taking advantage of every opportunity he could find to speak publicly.

Some semblance of psychological safety is important. The idea is not to get people to do *wildly* uncomfortable things, just *willfully* uncomfortable things. They need to know that you're asking them to do uncomfortable things to promote their growth and career advancement. To make this work, you need to know your employees' goals, aspirations, and areas for needed growth and provide uncomfortable opportunities that promote those aims. For example, if you've got a painfully introverted worker who also aspires to be a leader, you might have that person lead the weekly status meeting in your absence. Conversely, if you've got an employee who's extroverted to the point of being offensive or oblivious about how everyone else perceives him, you might have him be the note taker at the same meeting, instructing the über-extrovert not to talk, only to listen and scribe. The opportunities you provide as leader should be outside of those areas where people already feel comfortably skilled.

ROLE MODEL: SEEK DISCOMFORT YOURSELF

People will also be much more willing to move toward discomfort if they see you do uncomfortable things too. When asked to comment on how risk taking had influenced his career, the division president of a large communications company put it this way: "Throughout my career, I've always been willing to take jobs that were outside of my skill set. Some people think that's crazy, but I'm telling you that I wouldn't be sitting here as president if I had done it any other way. It's dangerous to be too safe. Look, even today I'm outside of my comfort zone. I'm an engineer, but I'm basically leading a sales organization. I knew next to nothing about sales before I took this job. Getting out of my comfort zone keeps me challenged. I want our people to do the same thing. They need to scrape their knees like I did, but knowing that I won't let them break their legs."

It's easier to get people to do uncomfortable things when you lead the way. There is no more powerful influencer of behavior in the workplace than the role modeling of the leaders. To this end, ask yourself what's the most uncomfortable thing you've done at work in the last three months. If you don't have a solid answer, maybe you're too comfortable. Here are some examples of minimally uncomfortable actions you can take to role model purposeful discomfort:

- Request to cover an agenda item at your boss's next status meeting.
- Make an apology to someone whose development you feel like you've been neglecting.
- Go to night school and take a certification class that's relevant to your job.
- Purposely solicit anonymous feedback about your leadership style and effectiveness by going through a 360-degree leadership-feedback process.

OPEN-DOOR ACTIONS AND REFLECTIONS:

- Use the boxes below to compare your answers to these two questions: Where are you playing it too safe in your career? What is the cost that too much safety is having on your career?

playing it safe	cost to career

- Now that you know where you're playing it too safe and what it's costing you, identify two or three specific courageous actions to move into discomfort. For each action, mark where on the comfort/discomfort continuum the action resides. Actions with a rating of 5 or less may not be courageous—or uncomfortable— enough!

Very comfortable   Very Uncomfortable

```
0    1    2    3    4    5    6    7    8    9   10
```

- Consider the degree of comfort your direct reports have in executing their job assignments. For each direct report, identify one purposefully uncomfortable skill-stretching task.

Doors of Opportunity

The chapters in the first section were about establishing an open-door leader mind-set. Leaders are most effective when they elevate people to a higher standard of performance by opening many doors of opportunity. Adopting an opportunity focus means viewing challenges as things to be expected, valued, and embraced. Moving others toward opportunity, however, also means purposefully nudging them out of comfort zones. Opportunities are uncomfortable things, and open-door leaders help people and organizations grow to the extent that they inspire them to do the uncomfortable.

This section builds upon the foundational principles covered in section I and introduces six unique doors that any aspiring open-door leader needs to know how to open.

In this section you'll learn

- why giving people something to prove is powerfully important,
- how open-door leadership often involves getting people to see the world differently,
- why second chances are important, and when to give them,
- why tapping into the perspectives of those who stand

outside the majority is critically important to your success as an open-door leader and to their success as employees,

- how open-door leaders can bring about personal transformation in themselves and others, and
- why open-door leadership requires opening your heart to those you lead.

CHAPTER 4

The Proving-Ground Door

One of the beautiful things about baseball is that every once in a while you come into a situation where you want to, and where you have to, reach down and prove something.
—Nolan Ryan

On any day between Memorial Day and Labor Day, Little League baseball games are underway at neighborhood ballparks throughout the land. While there's no guarantee which team will win, be it the Johnsonville Juggernauts or the Midville Mudslingers, what *is* guaranteed is that at least one little bench-sitting baseball player will be pleading with his coach from the sidelines, "Put me in, Coach! I'm ready to play!"

Every kid who plays baseball dreams of making a big play or hitting a home run. But it takes being given a shot, and it's the coach who decides who gets to step up to the plate.

Adults are like kids, just with bigger clothes and bigger egos. We want a chance to shine. We want to prove—to ourselves and to others—what we can do. But our chance to shine hinges on whether we get a proving ground where we can test our mettle. Often, unless our leader opens a door to an opportunity proving ground, our skills will languish or we will go unnoticed among our teammates.

Few things are as motivating as having something to prove. It is what propels the entrepreneurial spirit that so many organizations are desperate to ignite. Open-door leaders are wise to take advantage of the deep-seated desire that human beings have to prove their worth. Often, the open-door leader is the only person with the keys to the proving-ground door.

Who Deserves an Opportunity?

Who, exactly, should the open-door leader provide with an opportunity? Why *everyone* of course! That said, opportunities are more urgently needed for a person who is

- early in her career and needs to prove her meddle,
- late in her career and needs a "swan song" assignment,
- suffering after a career setback and needs to prove herself *to* herself in order to reclaim her confidence,
- hungry to exercise and showcase her latent skills so she can advance,
- ready to jump onto the management track,
- long overdue for a good opportunity, having earned the right to have her moment to shine,
- slotted to succeed a beloved senior executive and in need of a substantial and visible "win" to gain loyalty, or
- a flight risk because she is underchallenged and thirsty to add more value and take on more responsibility.

SMALL PROVING BEFORE BIG PROVING

As an open-door leader, you have to dole out opportunities in absorbable doses. Otherwise you may inadvertently set people up for failure. Often the best way to prepare someone for a big opportunity is to give him or her a number of smaller, lead-up opportunities. In other words, little doors come before big doors.

Early in my career, I worked for an experiential team-building company called Executive Adventure (EA). Based in Atlanta, EA provides spirited team-development services, often involving experiential activities. I had learned about EA in an in-flight magazine article just after completing my graduate studies in organizational development. This was the kind of company any guy in his late twenties would want to join! The work involved putting groups of corporate execs through fun team-building obstacles in scenic outdoor locations. Some of the obstacles, commonly called "ropes courses," were suspended forty feet in the air. Particularly attractive was the fact that I wouldn't have to wear a business suit, just rugged outerwear.

I was hired into the company in a sales position. Though it wasn't the position that I was hoping for, I figured that it was a good way to get my foot in the door until an opportunity emerged for me to move into a facilitator position.

Bob Carr, the founder of the company and a pioneer in corporate team building, was very aware of my desire to move into the role of team-building facilitator. He knew my educational background and my career aspirations. Still, since I was a newcomer to the profession, he couldn't risk having me facilitate sessions for EA's high-profile clients, which included Delta Airlines, Coca-Cola, Prudential Insurance, the Home Depot, and many other renowned companies. After all, how could a young buck like me offer guidance on how to be a strong team to people who had been working on teams for many more years than I had? At the same time, I would never be able to provide such guidance if I never got the chance to work with the corporate groups. I was stuck in the proverbial need-experience-to-get-experience catch-22.

Each year, EA did a number of projects for nonprofit organizations. While nonprofits deserved, and got, the same quality programs as our for-profit clients, working for nonprofits came with less pressure. Plainly, executives working in nonprofits were less uptight than their corporate counterparts, who often exhibit aggressive and sometimes cutthroat competition. Nonprofits thrive to the extent that they build cooperative alliances with funders, policy makers, and other stakeholders. Also, most nonprofits are focused on delivering programs and services (or creating opportunities) for people who are less fortunate. They tend to be socially conscious. So execs in nonprofits are generally more forgiving than their for-profit counterparts.

Knowing that the risk of upsetting the client with a rookie facilitator was lower, Bob gave me my first shot at facilitating a group while working with a nonprofit. Like the other facilitators, I received a briefing about the goals of the event from the client. Like the other facilitators, I knew which activities we were going to do and what learning points we aimed to draw out during the facilitated discussions after each team-building activity. Unlike the other facilitators, however, I had no facilitation experience. Knowing this, as I worked with my assigned group, Bob was always within earshot of the group and me.

More than twenty years later, I can still see Bob's face with a satisfied "the kid's got promise" grin. He saw raw potential in my unrefined skills as a facilitator. Not long after the project, he gave me another nonprofit assignment and then another and another still. Eventually, I got the chance to work with for-profit corporate groups too.

All of my early work with EA became a proving ground where my skills got sharper and my confidence grew. So much of this had to do with the things Bob did as an open-door leader for me. He was very hands-on. He would set aside time with me after each workshop. He would ask me to critique myself and then provide me with his own candid feedback. He suggested more impactful ways to word my questions. He shared stories about mistakes he had made along the way and what those mistakes taught him. Finally, he frequently pointed out the progress I was making but often couldn't see myself. All of these things helped me become more confident. But they also helped Bob become more confident in me, culminating in his asking me to take over EA's largest client contract, with the Ford Motor Company. The program involved conducting twenty-seven team-building programs for Ford's New Employee Orientation (NEO) program at their world headquarters in Dearborn, Michigan. I would be responsible for leading a team of seven other EA facilitators and would be Ford's key point of contact.

My proving ground with Ford turned out to be a true field of play. I was responsible for designing a scenario-based business-simulation activity that involved having teams of new Ford engineers build cars out of PVC pipe and then race them against each other. The work was challenging and mentally stimulating and required the full use of my imagination. The client held me to high standards, demanded solid work, and could be "Ford Tough." The entire experience made me a better and more capable professional.

Remember that I started out at EA as a sales guy. But with the support of Bob, a hands-on open-door leader, I received proving opportunities to grow, develop, and progress. The work with Ford remains one of the highlights of the early part of my career and culminated with my being named vice president at Executive Adventure. Eventually, I was facilitating more EA programs than even Bob himself was. Working with Bob convinced me of the value of opening doors for the people you lead.

THE FOUR HALLMARKS OF OPEN-DOOR LEADERSHIP REVISITED

Bob, my former boss, is a good example of an open-door leader. The approach he used in helping me grow professionally illustrates the four skills that a leader needs to open doors of opportunity. Though these skills were introduced in chapter 1, it is worth revisiting each skill to reinforce how essential they all are to open-door leadership. Let's briefly walk through each skill using Bob's approach in opening this door as an example:

- **Knowing Your Employees:** Even when I was hired on as a salesperson, Bob knew that my aspiration was to facilitate team-building programs. He knew that for me to grow and progress, he would have to create a path out of my entry-level sales role and into the role that I desired. Knowing your employees' ambitions and where they hope to end up will ensure that you fit them for the right opportunity.
- **Matching Suitedness:** After I proved to Bob and myself that I was capable of facilitating more consequential programs, Bob saw the connection between my skills and capabilities and the outcomes our client (Ford) was trying to achieve. He knew that I was well suited to lead the job. Open-door leaders match a person's skills (or lack thereof) with the opportunities that can make him or her stronger. As will be explained later, even a person's prior failure can be an indicator that he or she is well suited for an opportunity.
- **Envisioning Desired Results:** Bob knew that if he gave me a smaller and less-consequential proving ground (by leading smaller nonprofit programs), my skills would become sharper and I would eventually add more value to our company and the clients we served. He had spent enough quality-development time with me to have a clear vision of the professional I was capable of becoming. Every assignment was a step down the path of helping me live into that vision.

- **Providing Ongoing Support:** Bob had a stake in supporting and promoting my success every step of the way. He actively coached me. He shared his favorite facilitator questions. He gave me feedback about my performance after soliciting my own. He and I attended client meetings together. His support helped me grow, and my growth benefited both the company and me. It's not enough to provide a person with an opportunity. You have to support them as they pursue the opportunity too.

For me, Bob was an open-door leader. When I look back on my career, I can connect the dots between my career as a management consultant today and the opportunities that Bob Carr gave me early on. While I may have been "a kid with promise," the promise would have gone unfulfilled if Bob had not given me small and large opportunity proving grounds.

The end result for me is deep gratitude. By opening a door to a proving ground, the open-door leader gains deep loyalty. It makes sense. After experiencing the proving ground, how could you not be grateful to the leader who gave you the access? How could you not be grateful to the leader who gave you your first shot?

Give Me a Break!

Creating other leaders is an essential responsibility of leadership. As a practical reality, the only way to do that is to give others a chance to lead. In other words, you've got to give people a break. People want, and need, opportunities to break away from the past, break free of their routines, break away from the herd, and break into the place that you've already reached.

There's a very strong connection between giving people a break and your legacy as a leader. Consider this list of famous comedians and try to figure out what they all have in common: David Letterman, Jay Leno, Tim Allen, Bill Maher, Roseanne

Barr, Joan Rivers, Drew Carey, Ellen DeGeneres, and Jerry Seinfeld. Did you get what—or more accurately *who*—they have in common?

The answer is Johnny Carson.

During Johnny's reign as the host of *The Tonight Show*, the goal of any up-and-coming comedian was to win Johnny's approval. If he liked your routine, he'd wink and give you the okay sign. If he *really* liked your act, he'd call you over to sit next to him for some banter. If you "killed" on *The Tonight Show*, your success was virtually assured, which is why comedians were so eager for the chance to prove themselves on Johnny's show. Johnny had an eye for comedic talent. He could spot the diamond in the rough, and he genuinely enjoyed giving budding comics their big break. Johnny opened doors for many comedians we continue to enjoy today. Johnny Carson was an open-door leader.

When you give someone a chance to prove herself, you validate that she is someone worth taking a chance on. Even if she fails, she will learn, grow, and progress in the process. That growth, whether the result of success or failure, will make her more likely to succeed in the future. Thus, as a leader, your job is to keep providing proving-ground opportunities, because that's where the growth happens.

OPEN-DOOR ACTIONS AND REFLECTIONS:

Think about the people you're currently leading or influencing at work and then respond to these questions and statements:

- How could you use your influence to create opportunities for them? Is there someone right now who could use a "break"?
- Is there someone who has been asking for a chance to take on greater challenges or responsibilities? How could you make that happen?
- What are some smaller opportunities you could offer

as preparation to bigger ones? What proving-ground doors could you open right now?

- Next, look back over the course of your career. List some people who "gave you a shot." Were there some smaller opportunities that they gave you that led to bigger ones? What doors opened for you because of the interest they took in you? What reflections and insights do you have from these leaders? Positive or negative?

- Drawing on the example you just listed, create a concentric opportunity map. Draw the small opportunities that you received at the bottom of the map and then larger ones leading up to the big opportunity.

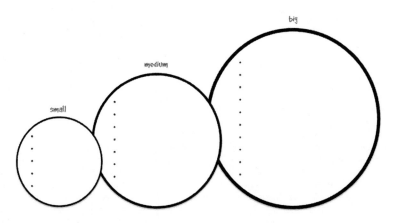

- Now think about someone you're currently leading. Start with the big opportunity you'd like to create for them. Work your way down through the map. What smaller opportunity could you create in the very near future?

- Review the four skills required of an open-door leader. What actions could you take to enhance your use of the four skills? What actions can you take, for example, to get to know the career aspirations of your direct reports better?

CHAPTER 5

The Thought-Shifting Door

Change your thoughts and you change your world.
—**Norman Vincent Peale**

Not all opportunities are tangible. Some are more mental in nature. In addition to providing people with tangible, skill-developing work opportunities, open-door leaders need to know how to shift people's thinking. Real opportunities can be found in getting people to be more imaginative by freeing them from narrow, negative, or habitual thinking.

This chapter introduces three aspects of bringing about thought shifts. The first involves catching people off guard by disrupting their mental routines. The second involves the use of symbolism, which can help shift people's focus back to the priorities that matter most. The third involves small language changes. There's a big difference between "not bad" and "pretty good." Small word choices make big differences in people's thoughts and attitudes.

USE A BARBEQUE IN THE PARK, NOT A CONFERENCE ROOM!

One challenge most leaders face is how to inspire more workplace creativity. There are plenty of clock punchers out there, folks who are physically working but mentally retired. Elevating people to higher standards of performance and inspiring useful ideas requires igniting their imaginations. Open-door leaders are keen to prevent complacency and lethargy. They know that mental grooves of habit eventually form ruts of routine. When people see things the way they've always seen them, everything stays the same, dulling work to the point of drudgery.

Inspiring creativity and imagination often requires disrupting people's mental routine and catching them off guard. For example, a large manufacturer of paper plates held a series of marketing meetings. For people who spent most of their working life centered on this commodity product, the way to reach more customers was pretty straightforward … discounting! Any time the company wanted to increase market share, they would just pump out more Sunday coupons. But the temporary discount-driven boost in market share would often come at the expense of lower profit margins. The division's leader needed people to be more imaginative than just defaulting to discounting all the time. He wanted people to remember that they weren't just selling plates, cups, and napkins. They were working for a brand that was deeply connected to the family experience.

To lift people out of the rut of discount thinking, he conducted a brainstorming meeting at a beautiful community park near the corporate headquarters. The meeting was different because it was set up as a backyard barbeque. There were picnic tables with red-and-white checkered tablecloths, an outdoor grill sizzling with hotdogs and hamburgers, even outdoor games like horseshoes and tetherball. Of course there was something else too: lots of the company's plates, cups, and napkins. They weren't just commodities; they were an essential part of the experience. The division's open-door leader had helped people shift their thinking away from commodities and toward *values* and *traditions*. The employees started seeing that on any summer day, their products were smack-dab in the middle of people's backyard barbeques, picnics, and family birthday parties. The company's products were important because they helped make people's family time more fun, enjoyable, and worry-free. Without the picnic table, grill, *and their products*, a backyard would just be a sorry patch of land behind the house.

Contrast this leader's approach to inspiring people's imagination with the one you've probably experienced. Your boss probably gathered people in the same old meeting room where people usually drone over monthly accounting reports. The meeting was held at 2:00 p.m., just as everyone's after-lunch coma was setting in. You probably had to hunt around in other parts of the building to find a flipchart and then went on a second hunt to find a marker that actually worked. Then, hoping to get lots of colorful ideas, your boss, standing next to a white piece of flipchart paper and holding a black marker, gleefully said, "Okay everyone, let's get creative!"

By choosing to get people outside of their thinking routines, away from the four-walled environment of their workplace, the division leader helped shift people's thinking for the better. When people started percolating on new marketing and product ideas, the word "discounting" never came up. Instead, they started talking about creative marketing campaigns designed to inspire the feelings of a warm summer afternoon. They talked about partnering with an outdoor grill company. They talked about new "summer flower" design borders for their plates and napkins. They talked about creating an interactive website where customers could swap their favorite picnic recipes. By shifting people's thinking and getting them away from the ordinary work environment, the open-door leader opened up a space for people to think in a more inspired way.

Host a Dinner Party at Pearl Harbor?

One of the most effective ways open-door leaders get people to think differently is by using *symbolism*. The CEO of a large fashion design company, for example, wanted to inspire more courageous behavior among the general managers who ran the company's retail stores. He was concerned that the company's very success could plant the seeds of complacency. The general managers had blown past their yearly sales goals, earning them a five-day trip to Hawaii, where the CEO decided to host the annual GM conference. To reinforce the dangers of getting caught off guard by complacency, the CEO hosted a dinner at Pearl Harbor … on the deck of the USS *Missouri*. The out-of-the-ordinary location of the meeting perfectly aligned, symbolically, with the message that he was aiming to send, that now was not the time to let up.

The "Mighty Mo" is one of the most famous battleships of all time. She joined the Pacific fleet after being christened by Harry Truman's daughter Margaret during World War II. She fought at Iwo Jima and Okinawa. She suffered, but withstood, a kamikaze attack. Later she fought in the Korean War, and still later in the Gulf War. Perhaps most famously, it was on the deck of the Mighty Mo where, in front of General Douglas MacArthur and Admiral Chester Nimitz, the Japanese signed the Instrument of Surrender.

There, under Mo's gigantic guns, the CEO thanked everyone for their hard work and reminded them about the importance of courage, persistence, and preventing complacency. Though they were very, very successful, the headwinds of competition were strong and unrelenting. Just as the Mighty Mo never surrendered in the face of hardship, neither should they. He showed them that they weren't just working for a fashion company. They were fighting in a fiercely competitive marketplace, and nothing short of their level best would keep sales in tip-top shape and preserve the company's rich tradition of success.

Symbols: You Weave the Meaning

Using symbols is a powerful way to help shift people's thinking. Open-door leaders have to speak about more than just the mechanics of the business. They have to show people how their jobs fit into a larger context. They have to be weavers of meaning and significance, helping people draw the connections between their seemingly small jobs and the more extraordinary purpose that they're helping advance. By providing symbolic reference points, open-door leaders help people view their world differently, animating people's souls and imaginations. Here are some other examples of this approach:

- A division head of a large international hotel chain hosts a series of small meetings in a hotel suite of their flagship location. The meetings focus on "owning the sleep market." A medical doctor who specializes in healthy sleep habits comes in to help them prompt new ideas.
- The leader of a creative consulting firm closes the business every March 4 so people can dedicate themselves to an idea that they find personally inspiring. They are encouraged to "march forth" toward their idea.
- The leader of a company that's aiming to transform its culture hosts a meeting at the Fernbank Museum of Natural History in Atlanta. A world-renowned cultural anthropologist speaks to the attendees about what strengthens and weakens cultures.
- Every other month, the director of career development of a large Chicago-based company hosts a small meeting to deepen the impact of the company's leadership-development program. Instead of meeting at his office, the gathering is held at the Catalyst Ranch, a creative venue designed for ideation and brainstorming meetings. Catalyst Ranch is like a Warholian psychedelic curio shop … but with flipcharts! The groovy atmosphere promotes imaginative "what-if" thinking. (Learn more at www. catalystranch.com.)

For a Better Result, Shift the Language

Shifting people's thinking doesn't require grandiose gestures on the part of the open-door leader. Sometimes just making small *language shifts* affects how people define themselves. For example, the owner of a $4 billion construction company wanted his division heads to do less managing and more leading. For decades, the division heads had been called business group *managers*. Was it really any wonder then that their focus was on *managing* their divisions? But the owner now needed them to focus less on internal operational issues (management) and more on external opportunities, such as developing business with clients (leadership). So he did something simple but important. He changed their job titles and, by definition, the expectation and focus of their jobs. Now the division heads are called business group *leaders*.

Opening Heads

Part of your job as an open-door leader is to keep people from thinking in ways that are counterproductive to themselves and the organization. You need to open the thought-shifting door. Catching people off guard and disrupting their mental routines, using symbols, and making small changes in language are great tools for shifting people's thinking. Surely there are other ways too. The means you use matter less than getting people to think positively, constructively, and productively.

Open-Door Actions and Reflections:

- What symbol or metaphor best resembles what your organization is trying to achieve through its work? How could you use this symbolic reference to communicate with people in a powerful or compelling way? Be specific in explaining how you'll use the symbol/metaphor.

- What are some ways that your organization typically tries to inspire creative ideas? What about the approach works well? What opportunities for improvement do you see?
- Use the first column of the framework below to identify a few one-word examples of unproductive or outdated thinking (e.g., "apathetic," "fearful"). In the second column, list the healthier and more productive words you'd like reflected in people's attitudes (e.g., "initiative," "courageous"). In the third column list actions that you could take to shift people from the first column to the second (e.g., "jointly set ambitious goals," "institute temporary job rotations"). Finally, and importantly, set a deadline for finishing each action!

Unproductive Thinking	Productive Thinking	Thought-shifting Actions	Action Deadline

CHAPTER 6

The Door to a Second Chance

Having a second chance makes you want to work even harder.
—Tia Mowry

The company's owner will neither confirm nor deny that he is Mr. Fusion. Many people think he is. Then again, maybe he isn't. But he sure could be. Maybe.

If he is Mr. Fusion, he is one of the most famous computer hackers in the world. He is part James Bond and part Mark Zuckerberg. He is in an elite group of coders who are capable of hacking into the most sensitive government systems. He did so singlehandedly.

Even if he isn't Mr. Fusion, he is deeply, deeply involved in cyber warfare. *BusinessWeek* called the company he founded the "premier cyber-arms dealer." The company expertise is *zero-day exploits*. That's geek-speak for being able to take advantage of computer software or application vulnerabilities that are unknown even to the software's own developers. His company is comprised of "white hat" hackers who develop code to exploit security holes to conduct international clandestine surveillance operations. Sometimes they will go further, conducting all-out cyber attacks against bad-guy nations. Be glad that they are on our side.

Mr. Fusion's company is into some wild, jaw-dropping stuff.

And some very important people sit on the company's board of directors—people whose names you would instantly recognize for their spy credentials or high military rank.

But Mr. Fusion, if he is Mr. Fusion, is only able to do what he does because an open-door leader gave him a second chance.

How Would You Handle a Hacker?

In 1989, during the first Gulf War, the Pentagon became increasingly concerned that foreign enemies or terrorist groups would exploit US defense systems. The concern was especially pronounced because they had caught a Washington, DC, teenager hacking into the air force's computer systems just days before Iraq invaded Kuwait. In the dark world of the hacker community, the kid was known only by his chat-room handle: Mr. Fusion.

Consider what you would do if you caught a teenage punk hacking into some of the most sensitive computer systems in the world—systems that, in the wrong hands, could destabilize the nation's security system, or worse. Would you throw the book at the delinquent, sending him to a maximum security prison for the rest of his life? Would you exact a stronger punishment—maybe expel him from the United States and set him up in a dank prison in the Czech Republic? Or would you think about the opportunities this "problem" child presented?

Think for a second about the unique skills that Mr. Fusion had acquired. Wouldn't you rather have these skills working for you instead of against you? What if you could replicate his skills? Or what if Mr. Fusion could make some introductions for you to other Mr. Fusions out there?

The key to being an open-door leader is finding the opportunity in situations that other people view as problems. Mr. Fusion breaking into the computer system of a military computer system was a problem, to be sure, on an international scale. But it was also a gigantic opportunity. Skills like his were exceedingly rare, but the uses for those skills, from a national security standpoint, were becoming increasingly numerous. Hackers are more imaginative, clever, and devious than graduates of computer science programs. Their talents are too exceptional to find through the traditional means of recruiting. Hackers aren't recruited; they're caught—but only rarely. And when you catch one, you have a decision to make: opportunity or punishment?

AN OPEN-DOOR LEADER STRIKES A DEAL

The open-door leader in this story is Special Agent Jim Christy, the chief of computer crime investigations with the air force's Office of Security Investigations at the time of the breach.[2] He struck a win/win deal with Mr. Fusion and shifted the situation from a problem to an opportunity. At the criminal sentencing, Christy would testify on Mr. Fusion's behalf. In exchange, Mr. Fusion would help the air force secure its computer systems by hacking into as many computers as he could. He would get to keep doing what he loved to do, just in a way that was constructive. He would shift from being a hacker to being a *cracker*, in the spirit of the code crackers of World War II. Christy would set him up with a workspace and with all the resources he needed to go to work.

With agents watching his every keystroke, within three weeks Mr. Fusion was able to breach more than two hundred air force systems. Eventually, using Mr. Fusion's methods and tools, along with skills from others in the hacker community, a government team of crackers were able to access 88 percent of *all* military systems. More importantly, with the system vulnerabilities now

---

2   "Sgt. Pat McKenna, Hacker Trackers Give Crackers a Bad Time: USAF OSI Makes Life Tuff for Script Kiddies." Article published in *Gulf Coast Computing* online magazine, accessed May 2012.

exposed, the systems could be made more secure. All this happened because Christy gave Mr. Fusion a second chance. Maybe.

STRATEGIC FORGIVENESS

The essence of a second chance is *strategic forgiveness*. This is not the forgiveness of a spiritual nature. It is the forgiveness of an opportunistic nature. It is the kind of forgiveness that, after weighing all of the factors and grievances, recognizes that the person who gets a second chance often becomes deeply loyal and deeply committed to walking on a nobler path. By giving a person a second chance, the open-door leader creates an opportunity for a conversion experience so the errant person can make healthier and more productive choices. While there is a risk of getting burned by giving a second chance, the opportunities outweigh the risk when you convert someone from destructive behavior to constructive behavior. Mr. Fusion's story extends beyond his helping the air force. If we are to believe the rumors, he is now a productive, tax-paying member of society whose clandestine company employs more than fifty "white hat" computer-hacking patriots who work for the good of national security.

WHEN A SECOND CHANCE IS WORTH THE RISK

An open-door leader has to be very thoughtful about when to give a second chance to someone. Giving an embezzler a second chance would be stupid, for example. Letting someone off the hook for sexual harassment would be immoral, not to mention get you both fired. So who does deserve a second chance? People who

- made an honest and legal mistake,
- approached the situation thoughtfully and logically but found that the outcome just didn't work out (good reasons, bad outcome),
- made the mistake out of ignorance, not malice— suchas a young employee who barges into the CEO's office to ask for a raise,

- suffer after a career setback but have a long track record of adding value to the company, or
- are deeply embarrassed for their mistakes and likely to retain the lesson for the duration of their careers.

ARE YOU A "NO CHANCE" LEADER?

Many leaders are quick to punish and slow to forgive. When workers make mistakes and beg for mercy, they say, "No way!" Then they rub the mistake maker's nose in the mistake, as if the person were an errant dog in need of punishment. It's as if they take pleasure in the role of punisher, reveling in leveling harsh judgments. Their power derives from their ability to cause pain.

Open-door leaders, conversely, are powerful because they opt first for mercy and use punishment only as a last-resort exception. By choosing forgiveness over iron-fisted punishment, the open-door leader creates a learning opportunity; the person who has been traveling down the wrong road stands the best chance of getting on the right path.

How do you handle it when an employee loses a client, gets the data wrong, comes in over budget, or drops the ball in some other way? Do you explode? Do you mentally write the person off for good and hold the mistake against him or her forever more? Do you stew with resentment? What kind of example are you setting for others by the way you handle (or mishandle) mistakes? While no leader should tolerate habitual mistakes, all leaders should expect some mistakes ... even from themselves. Mistakes, small and big, often provide the best learning opportunities. The learning vanishes, however, if the punishment far outweighs the mistake.

OPEN-DOOR ACTIONS AND REFLECTIONS:

- Think of a time when you made a mistake. What was it? How did people label you after you made it? Who gave you a second chance along the way? How did the second chance impact who you are today?

- How do you handle or mishandle mistakes? What was the most recent mistake that one of your direct reports made? Were you able to turn the mistake into a learning opportunity? How did you do it?

- Have you been harboring a resentment or grudge against someone at work? What would it take for you to forgive him or her? What might be the benefits—to him or her and to you—that might make forgiveness a strategic choice?

Chapter 7

Opening Doors for Others

I believe that we are here for each other, not against each other.
Everything comes from an understanding that you are a gift
in my life—whoever you are, whatever our differences.
—John Denver

Opening doors for others is an essential job of any leader. But leaders don't treat all *others* equally, unfortunately. Leaders have a tendency to promote people who are just like them in gender, ethnicity, sexual orientation, and disposition. It's just plain easier to develop a common bond and kinship with people who look like, talk like, and think like you do. It's also just plain dangerous.

While gravitating toward members of one's own tribe is understandable, when leaders surround themselves with duplicates, cliques form, groupthink takes over, and outside *others* get resentful and restless. Worse, when leaders exclude *others*, they also exclude the varied perspectives and ideas that could help the leaders make better and more imaginative decisions. And just who are these *others* the leader is excluding? Anyone who doesn't fit the predominant profile of the folks at the top. People from outside the dominant tribe.

The vast majority of senior leaders across nearly all organizations throughout the United States and Europe are white men. That's not an indictment. It's just a fact. The challenge is that it's not a natural act for male white leaders to open doors for women, blacks, other nonwhites, people with disabilities, or homosexuals. Excluding these *others* from the top ranks likely has less to do with duplicity or racism (at least consciously) than it does with obliviousness and ignorance. Yet the impact is the same. Qualified people never get a fair chance to succeed, which harms both them and the organization.

Them's Not like Us

Many leadership-development programs focus on next-level leaders and are designed to develop the bench strength of the folks who will someday be running the organization—high-potential successors. The best of these programs involve a rigorous intake process: bosses nominate program candidates, who then complete surveys and assessments before they audition for inclusion in the program. Yet regardless of how objective and rigorous the intake process is, often the selected candidates resemble the very people who nominated them in the first place—their leaders. When this happens—and it happens a lot—the most senior leaders would be wise to cast a wider net to include less obvious high-potential candidates. Otherwise they are in danger of replicating themselves, losing the advantages that differing perspectives can yield.

To be clear, most leaders are not consciously racist or bigoted. My experience working with many leaders has been largely the opposite. Most are decent and ethical people. They just default to creating duplicates at the top. So they need a lot of reminders—from shareholders, advocacy groups, outside consultants, etc.—to include *others*. Including less-obvious candidates during the screening process lowers the risk of missing a talented gem who could have shined as a leader.

OPEN-DOOR LEADERS CREATE OPPORTUNITIES FOR WOMEN

Without active and intentional support from leaders, especially male white leaders, the opportunity landscape for *others* is much smaller and restricted. According to the White House Project Report[3] for example, worldwide, women make up roughly 52 percent of the labor market. Yet they only account for about 18 percent of top leadership positions across industry sectors in the United States, despite the fact that almost 90 percent of the general public consistently reports being comfortable having women in top leadership roles. What makes this disparity particularly troublesome is that according to a recent, though controversial, study of 7,280 leaders conducted by Zenger Folkman and featured in the *Harvard Business Review*,[4] women often outperform their male counterparts in top-level jobs. The study suggests that any organization that cares about profits and performance would be well served to include more women at the top.

To be sure, women have made great strides in cracking the proverbial glass ceiling. The CEO of IBM is a woman (Ginny Rometty). But while the glass ceiling isn't as solid as it used to be, it still exists. History suggests that women will not be able to fully dismantle the ceiling by sheer force of will and talent without the active contribution and cooperation of male leaders. The reality is that men largely hold the keys to the boardroom and C-suite. So if they aren't actively creating opportunities for women—a very large group of *others*—male leaders run the risk of becoming opportunity obstructionists.

---

3   The White House Project Report: Benchmarking Women's Leadership, 2009, http://www.benchmarks.thewhitehouseproject.org.

4   J. Zenger and J. Folkman, "Are Women Better Leaders Than Men?" HBR Blog Network, http://blogs.hbr.org/cs/2012/03/a_study_in_leadership_women_do.html.

One difference between men and women at work is that a man can climb the corporate ladder based on hard work, ambition, and merit with very few obstructions. There's almost nothing stopping him if he's effective enough. Women can demonstrate all these attributes and still find diminishing opportunities as they progress, through no fault of their own. At that point, candidly, a woman may not get any farther without a man opening a door for her. This isn't paternalism. I am not suggesting that women are weak damsels who need men to rescue them. I *am* suggesting that by being overly attentive to their own tribe, male leaders routinely, and often unconsciously, obstruct opportunities for women by treating them as *others*.

Being an open-door leader means giving special attention to opening doors for *others* who are not like you. The good news is that there are some positive role models to follow. Andrea Jung, the former CEO and current board chair of Avon, for example, credits James Preston, her predecessor, with opening the C-suite door to her.[5] During her first interview with Preston, she noticed that there was an interesting plaque behind his desk. It bore four footprints: an ape, a barefoot man, a wingtip shoe, and a high-heeled shoe. Its title was "The Evolution of Leadership."

Jung is not alone in being an *other* who benefited from the progressiveness of an open-door leader. In a *USA Today*[6] survey of thirty-four female CEOs, thirty-three mentioned a man when asked to identify the mentor who had the most influence on their career. Interestingly, the common thread that most of these men share is having daughters. Greg Palmer, who mentored Jill Ater, founder of a company called 10 till 2, explains, "Having daughters, seeing firsthand their struggles, fears and dreams, it makes it easier to relate to other women and their struggles, fears

---

5   Del Jones, "Often, men help women get to the corner office," *USA Today*, August 5, 2009.

6   Ibid.

and dreams."[7] Palmer has three daughters, which seems to be a factor in making the *other* less "other."

FROM ONE MAN TO AN *OTHER*

Otherness diminishes rapidly when you can relate to the other's plight. Consider Marshall Carter, the past chair of the New York Stock Exchange and mentor to Deborah Ellinger, president of Restoration Hardware. In addition to having two daughters, Carter is a Vietnam vet, a former marine, and a recipient of the Navy Cross. When he returned home and sought employment after two tours as an officer in Vietnam, eighty-five companies rejected him, despite his master's degree in operations research and systems analysis. His stellar resume made no difference; the public's distaste for the war had turned him into an *other*.

As mentioned in chapter 2, an open-door leader sees opportunities where everyone else sees problems. Having experienced firsthand the humiliation of being obstructed from opportunities for which he was qualified, Carter was determined to not block opportunities for *others* who worked for him. Even in the early 1980s, when he was a senior executive at Chase Manhattan Bank, nine of the twelve vice presidents who reported to him were women. Summing up Carter's open-door leadership approach, Restoration's Ellinger says, "He understands what it means to be an outsider."[8]

EVEN *OTHERS* HAVE *OTHERS*

Each of us has an *other* somewhere in our lives. *Others* are members of minority groups. Not minority solely as in "black or Latino" but as in the minority within your own organization. *Others* are those people who represent a much smaller percentage of people within your organization. Just as the needs and concerns of a

---

7   Ibid.

8   Ibid.

woman working in a male-dominated workplace are unique, so too are those of a male worker working in a female-dominated workplace. The same holds true for an older employee working in a tech start-up company, surrounded by thumb-tapping, text-sending millennials. In each case, the non-*other* leader needs to pay special attention to make sure that doors are opening for all people, not just people who are just like the leader herself.

The challenge in leading *others* is that often *you don't know what you don't know*. Unless you directly seek out *other's* perspective, input, and feedback, you won't even know what their unique needs and concerns are and it will be hard to create opportunities for them. It's surprisingly easy to do. Just move *toward* them. Read blogs and newsletters that are written for these groups. Find out what causes they champion. Listen to podcasts from luminaries they respect. Most importantly, and to prevent stereotyping, spend time getting to know the individuals you're leading, even if their lives are very different from your own. Don't be interrogative. Just follow your curiosity and ask questions in the way a five-year-old would … innocently and with purity of heart.

A good example of spending time getting to know rank-and-file workers comes from BJ Gallagher, author of *Peacock in the Land of Penguins*, one of the best books ever written about working with *others*. During her years as the manager of training and development at the *Los Angeles Times,* she worked for a senior executive named Tom Johnson. BJ was teaching an evening workshop to the pressmen who worked at night printing the newspaper. Suddenly, at about 10:00 p.m., Tom Johnson popped into the room and said, "What's going on in here tonight? How's everybody doing?" The pressmen were happy to see him, and BJ was totally surprised. Keep in mind that Tom wasn't just *a* senior executive, he was *the* senior executive … the newspaper's publisher. Yet here he was at ten o'clock at night making small talk with the rank-and-file pressmen.

After Tom left, BJ asked the guys, "Does he do that often?" And they said, "Yes, he does. He often comes by late at night, after he's been to some corporate evening event, or the theater, or some business dinner. He comes in, picks up a copy of the paper as it's coming off the press, and talks with the guys for a while before he goes home."

One has to imagine that Tom, who would go on to become president of CNN for more than a decade, benefited from those meetings with *others* as much as they did. It was he, after all, who was the true *other*. In any company, the CEO is a minority of one. And too many leaders at the top cloister themselves in the executive suites, where the rarefied air can distance them from the people who do the actual work. Few things are as dangerous for a leader as becoming out of touch with their people's needs and wants. Open-door leaders like Tom Johnson, however, strive to tear down whatever walls exist between them and their workforce. When they do, *other*ness becomes less important than togetherness.

Open-Door Actions and Reflections:

- Identify a time in your career when you felt like an *other*. Describe the situation and the emotions that come up for you when you recollect it. Ultimately, how was this situation resolved? Did someone play the role of open-door leader in this situation? If so, what opportunity did they create for you? How could you pay that door-opening forward?
- Identify two colleagues who are *others* to you. Pick one person from each gender. Take each person to lunch, separately, simply to get to know him or her better. Afterward, see if there are some doors that would be worth opening for him or her.
- If your organization has a diversity office or function, spend an hour getting educated about what the organization is doing to create a level playing field for *others*. Review the data and statistics about the

composition of your workforce, including the top team and the board of directors. Meet with the diversity manager to ask how you can contribute toward the organization's diversity goals.

CHAPTER 8

The Door to Personal Transformation

*When we quit thinking primarily about ourselves
and our own self-preservation, we undergo a truly
heroic transformation of consciousness.*
—Joseph Campbell

Some executives think that leadership is only about momentum and results. But even a slave master can crack the whip hard enough to get people working harder and faster. The best leaders do more than move us forward. They also help us rise above who we are so that we can move closer to the person we can become. Open-door leaders uplift us. They elevate our standards, ethics, and performance by creating opportunities for us to transform ourselves.

Human growth and development require constantly advancing from who you are to who you want to become. Doing that requires that you discover who you truly are, and for most people, this is a big challenge. But how can you even know what to transform about yourself if you don't know who you are? Open-door leaders promote personal transformation by helping us know ourselves better, by holding us accountable to our own potential, and sometimes by hitting us upside the head with a left hook of reality. The most powerful means of promoting personal transformation, though, is through the examples they set for us as role models.

ROLE MODELING PERSONAL TRANSFORMATION

There is no more powerful influencer on the culture of a workplace than the behavior of its leaders. Leaders set the behavioral tone of the organization. For this reason, it's important for leaders to keep themselves evolving and growing. This means purposefully doing things that make themselves uncomfortable and creating opportunities for their own development. It's much easier to follow people who embody the values they are asking us to live up to.

Consider Cal, who inherited a multimillion-dollar business upon the sudden death of his father. Being only in his late twenties, and under intense pressure to not let the business fail, Cal overcompensated for his lack of leadership experience through heavy-handed and authoritarian leader behavior. Hundreds of people's livelihoods, he thought, were depending on his not failing. He was full of fear and transmitted that fear to others in the form of harsh leadership.

It's hard to get through to a hardhead. In Cal's case, getting through came in the form of a 360-degree leadership-feedback survey. Exhausted from his work pressures and perplexed by the frustrations of leading the company, Cal had signed up to attend a 7 Habits class at the Sundance Resort. The class would be led by Dr. Stephen Covey himself. Covey, of course, was the author of *The 7 Habits of Highly Effective People*, one of the most influential leadership books of all time.

The feedback Cal got was startling, especially the raw, qualitative comments at the end. Words like "dominating," "obnoxious," and "offensive" jumped off the page. Curiously, one word came up over and over: *afraid*. That word, in particular, stung. It stung because Cal knew that it was true. But he thought he had hid his fear with his commanding presence. Clearly, he hadn't hidden anything. And the 360 provided the proof.

Sometimes the best thing that can happen to a leader is for him or her to experience humiliation. Humiliation is the birthplace of humility. The embarrassment and shame that Cal felt tenderized his hardness. He was now ready to accept that he needed help, that he couldn't just *will* success into being. He was failing. Not because he wasn't working hard enough, but because he wasn't bringing people with him.

Cal set out to be a better leader. After attending the Covey program, he became a certified Covey instructor and brought the concepts back to his company. Other senior executives got certified too and, along with Cal, personally led workshops for the entire workforce. Other training opportunities were created too, and the training budget was dramatically increased. And, after conducting a series of focus groups to get the input of the workforce, the company created its first-ever mission statement.

Cal had changed for the better, and people could see it. He dictated less and asked for input more. He spent time talking about the company's strategy and the opportunities the strategy was focused on creating. He walked the halls and dropped in on people, just to see how things were going. He also said, "Thank you" ... a lot.

As Cal changed, so did the climate of the workplace. Work was still work, and the work had to get done. But it was getting done with enthusiasm and positive energy, not foot dragging and bellyaching. Cal's optimism had given way to a general workplace optimism. The company simply became a more positive place to be.

INSPIRING YOUR OWN PERSONAL TRANSFORMATION

It's hard to be an open-door leader if your mental door is closed. Transformation, personally and organizationally, needs to start with you. Here are some ways, ranging from conventional to nonconventional, to bring about your own life and leadership transformation.

- Get a mentor inside the organization and hire a coach outside the organization.
- Go through a 360-degree feedback process.
- Devise and recite a daily mantra, like "calm confidence," "be courageous," "discomfort equals growth," etc.
- Write a gratitude list at the start of each day.
- Sign up to do regular service work, like joining Big Brothers Big Sisters, building a house with Habitat for Humanity, etc.
- Start each day with five minutes of silent meditation.
- Take a yearly retreat at a transformational learning center, like the Esalen Institute at Big Sur, California.
- Change your insides by first changing your outsides—get an image makeover, change your clothes, hairstyle, etc.
- Experience this great big world by traveling abroad, alone.
- Get a personal trainer and/or sign up for a rigorous fitness program.
- Take a three-month sabbatical and get reacquainted with the you you always wanted to be.

Holding the Door Open

Sometimes opening the door for transformation is simply a matter of pointing a person in the direction of their potential and holding steady until he or she reaches it. A good example is the story of Steve, a project manager in a large commercial building company. Steve had enjoyed a successful career and was poised for a bright future. But then he suffered a crisis of confidence. A project that he had led tanked and lost millions of dollars. There were a host of reasons the project went south, including misestimating the cost of the work and underbidding the project, performing the work in an entirely new market, and a fickle and unreasonable client. If anything, Steve's leadership had prevented the project from being a bigger loss than it turned out to be. But he didn't view it that way. He personalized the failure. As a result, he started to doubt himself and became much more hesitant and much less confident.

Fortunately, Steve worked for a seasoned open-door leader. Wayne, Steve's boss, had experienced this same type of crisis earlier in his career. He knew what Steve was going through. Steve, he could tell, wanted to scale back his career a bit, become less visible, maybe take on smaller projects for a while. Wayne knew, from his own experience, what Steve really needed was to take on another large and complex project. Why? For two reasons. First, if Steve allowed himself to shrink, he might get comfortable with a lower standard of achievement. Second, Wayne knew that Steve was capable of so much more than he had even shown at this point. Wayne believed in Steve's potential even more than Steve did. If there's one thing grey-haired leaders eventually gain a keen eye for, it's talent. Despite the recent setback, Wayne knew that Steve was a really talented guy.

So what did Wayne do? He put Steve in charge of a large, complex project the company had just landed. The project was one of the largest in the company's history, and a *lot* of money was at stake. If that weren't enough, the project involved joint venturing with a partner that had no prior history with Steve's company. Oh yeah, and the project was on the opposite side of the country.

Notice that what made Steve suited for the new opportunity wasn't that he had been successful before. It was the opposite. He was suited for the opportunity because of his recent *failure* and the need to overcome it.

Steve pleaded with Wayne to pick someone else. Wayne listened patiently and then said, "No." Steve complained that he might lose the company money. Wayne said, "You'd better not." Steve said the move would be tough on his family. Wayne said, "Bring 'em." Steve said, "I'm afraid." Wayne said, "You should be."

Once you open a door of opportunity for somebody, you may have to keep him or her from closing it. Wayne knew that what Steve really needed was *redemption*—in the eyes of his company, but more importantly, in his view of himself. Steve would never hold himself accountable to who he was capable of becoming as a professional if Wayne let him settle for becoming a smaller self. Leaders fail. It comes with the territory. If anything, Wayne believed, Steve had earned a stripe that he hadn't yet claimed. Leading a big, hairy, complex job would be just what Steve needed to capitalize on the lessons he had learned from his prior failure. So Wayne refused to let Steve close the door. He kept Steve accountable to his own potential.

It's important to know that Wayne didn't just dump the opportunity in Steve's lap and then cut and run. Wayne was deeply involved every step of the way. Steve didn't take over the leadership helm instantaneously. There was some baton passing that had to happen first. Wayne and Steve worked closely together in shaping the relationship with the new venture partner. They jointly sifted through the project contract and estimates. They jointly attended client meetings. They traveled to, and presented at, the quarterly division meetings back at the company headquarters. They were in it together. Steve's opportunity to reclaim his confidence was

Wayne's opportunity to leave a positive and lasting imprint on a future leader.

By not letting up and by always being on point, Steve slowly reclaimed his confidence. As of the writing of this book, he is successfully leading the large joint venture. And Wayne is working on landing an even bigger project in the same area with Steve's help.

WAYS TO INCREASE ACCOUNTABILITY

Accountability is an all-or-nothing proposition. Either you are or you aren't. Your job as an open-door leader is to create an environment where everyone, including you, holds him or herself accountable. Here are some tips for increasing accountability in yourself and others.

- Write down explicit expectations about the activities, deliverables, and deadlines that have to be achieved; no vagaries allowed.
- List all the excuses you can think of for why the work won't get done; then list actions to remedy those excuses upfront.
- Clarify the rewards for success and the consequences for failure.
- Post the expectations in a place where they can continuously be seen and referred to.
- Make sure everyone is aware of each other's specific assignments—create social pressure to succeed.
- Establish a schedule of frequent progress reviews— increase the frequency if progress slips.
- After all of the activities, deliverables, and deadlines have been met (or not), conduct a lessons-learned meeting to capture improvement ideas for future assignments.

Could You Be a Velvet Hammer?

One of the most effective ways of increasing the likelihood of a personal transformation in others is to give straightforward feedback. Open-door leaders give us the kind of feedback that takes courage to deliver and even more courage to hear, and personal transformation is almost impossible without it. Consider, for example, this story of a middle manager whose boss, one of the most respected people in the company, gave him some hard-hitting feedback that most people wouldn't have the courage to give. One of the reasons everyone admired and respected the boss was his way of being a *velvet hammer*—he could deliver feedback in a way that would make you pay attention without putting up your defenses. During the middle manager's performance review, after talking about all of the things that he was doing well, his boss said, "There is one more thing that I have to tell you before you go. There's something that I'm just starting to notice, and I'm concerned that others will start to notice too. It can become a real drag on your career unless you deal with it. You're becoming a brown noser."

Ouch! Humiliated, the manager did what any brown noser would do: he tried to laugh it off. "What do you mean, boss? By the way, I meant to tell you that I really like your new tie!" But his boss didn't laugh. He wouldn't let this conversation drift into the shallow waters. And what the boss said next made all the difference: "Listen, you don't have to laugh at my jokes harder than they are funny. That's not only dishonest; it's manipulative. If you just agree with everything I say you'll be of no real value to me. You're a smart guy with a strong imagination. Rely on your own creativity and ideas to get ahead, not on kissing up to people like me."

Ten years after receiving the hard-to-hear feedback, the middle manager considers it the single most important conversation he had in his entire career. Essentially because his boss gave him permission to care less about what others thought about him.

He had been a people pleaser since he was a kid, not because he genuinely cared about others but because he liked being liked. By pleasing you, he could get you to like him, and if he could get you to like him, he might be able to get you to do what he wanted you to do ... for him. His boss's tough feedback helped shift him from unconfident inauthenticity to confident authenticity. It helped him become more of a truth-teller, which is supremely important to career advancement. After getting feedback about the error of his schmoozer ways, he learned to assert his opinions and ideas in a more muscular way. It's a transformational shift that has been critical to the development and advancement of his career.

Some people pride themselves on being *brutally* honest. But brutality almost always just puts up people's defenses. What matters most for the open-door leader is to provide feedback in a way that *gets through* to someone so he or she can put the feedback to work. The balance is one of assertiveness and diplomacy. Before delivering tough feedback, be thoughtful about what you want to say so that your words will meet with reception and not defensiveness. The feedback has to be absorbable and digestible in order to transform a person's behavior. The point of being a *velvet hammer* is not to make the person feel ashamed of him or herself or afraid of you. The point is to communicate assertively and respectably so that the other person benefits from the feedback.

How a Follower Made Me a Leader

Being a boss does not make one a leader, at least in the sense of an open-door leader. When it comes to creating opportunities for personal transformation, the term "leader" has less to do with hierarchy and more to do with the influence you bring to bear on people and situations. With a little courage, anyone at any level can be a leader. In the preface I mentioned that my journey toward becoming a leadership-development practitioner began when a courageous employee told me what a lousy leader I was.

He told me after I had pushed him to the point that he was set to quit.

I was the show director of an aquatic stage and stunt show put on by the US High Diving Team. Both the employee and I were also high divers in the show. Each day, our job was to climb a hundred-foot-high dive ladder and hurl ourselves toward the pool below, rushing down at speeds in excess of fifty miles per hour into a pool that was ten feet deep. In addition to performing our death-defying dives, often in front of crowds of two thousand people, we also performed Olympic-style dives, a comedy routine, and dangerous double-dive stunts. I'm not being overly dramatic when I tell you that on any day we could be killed on the job.

One day, after what I considered a subpar performance, I ripped into the team like General Patton. I told them that only chumps could put on a show like that. I told them that if they couldn't get with the program, I'd ditch them for divers who could. I told them that they made me ashamed to be their boss. Then I told them to get out of my face because looking at them disgusted me.

After my little tirade, one of the divers stayed behind. He looked me straight in the eye and said, "Listen, Treasurer, who do you think you are? Where do you get off talking to us like that? Do you think that by berating us and making us feel small you will earn our respect? All you do is harp on everyone's mistakes. What's your goal, dude? To make us afraid of you? At what cost? People hate working for you. If you talk to us like that again, I'll walk. I respect myself too much to let you treat me that badly."

The truth only hurts if it should. Hearing the employee's words was painful, because I knew down deep that he was right. I wasn't being a leader; I was being a jerk. The truth was that I had no confidence as a leader at all. I had no idea how to lead, so I adopted the style of my previous boss, and the boss before that. I adopted the most heavy-handed aspects of the leaders that I had experienced, all the way back up to my first leader role model: my father. I was basically channeling my dad, or at least my dad when he was angry. I had no idea who I was, authentically, as a leader. My employee's words confronted me with that reality. But it was exactly what I needed to prompt me to take an interest in the concept of leadership.

Few people have the courage to give their boss upward feedback. Respecting authority is one of our earliest lessons. So, faced with an abhorrent boss, most people bite their tongue, which enables the abhorrent behavior. In this case, however, the employee had gotten to the tipping point. The risk of telling me the hard truth on the ever-so-slim chance that I might actually change was less dangerous than letting me stay a world-class jackass. His courage in giving me the raw feedback that I needed to hear (but cringed at hearing) helped cause a personal transformation in me. It caused me to reflect on the leader I had been and desired to be. I started reading books on leadership and team building and got better results out of my team. I came across the term "organizational development" and decided to pursue a graduate degree in that subject. I wrote my thesis on leadership, which gave me my first taste of writing a book-sized manuscript. I can draw a very straight line from the uncomfortable but courageous feedback that diver gave me back then to the book that you're reading at this moment. In a very direct way, that feedback resulted in the life I live today as a leadership writer, speaker, and consultant. Without his courage, there's a very good chance that I would have gone on to other leadership roles in other organizations, doing a lot of damage to many people. His feedback became my opportunity to change ... for the better. Though I was his boss, he served as an open-door leader to me. The raw feedback he gave me instigated my personal transformation.

Open-Door Leaders Move Us toward Our Better Selves

Socrates advised us to "know thyself." It is, of course, very good advice, because it is hard to change yourself if you have no idea who you really are. But knowing yourself and transforming yourself based solely on introspection is next to impossible. Open-door leaders serve us best when they help us see ourselves in a different way. By being a good role model, opening the doors to allow us to experience transformation, holding us accountable to our own potential, and giving us direct and diplomatic feedback, they help us transform ourselves from the person we are to the person we're capable of becoming.

OPEN-DOOR ACTIONS AND REFLECTIONS:

- Identify at least one leader who helped bring about a personal shift for you. What was the shift? Why did you need it? What did the leader do to help bring it about?
- List the names of a few people who might consider you an open-door leader. What shifts would they say you helped bring about for them?
- Think back to a time in your career when someone gave you tough feedback. What did they say to you? How did you react? In what ways did this feedback impact you?
- Identify one person who needs some feedback that you've been avoiding giving. Why are you avoiding it? What shift might your feedback help that person make? How could you deliver the feedback in a way that preserves the dignity of the person yet still gets the point across? How could you be a "velvet hammer"?

CHAPTER 9

The Door to Your Open Heart

The minute a person whose word means a great deal to others dares to take the open-hearted and courageous way, many others follow.
—Marian Anderson

Do you care about me? This is what people want to know when they work for you. They may not say it directly, but it is the core question that defines the relationship between you and the people you lead. When people believe the answer is "yes," they will be more committed to their work ... and to you. But when they think the answer is "no," their commitment to their jobs and their loyalty to you will suffer.

To be a leader means to get results. But when the drive for results monopolizes a leader's attention, people become a lesser priority. When a leader cares more about the "ends" (results) and less about the "means" (people), the leader becomes susceptible to treating people like objects. You'll hear it in the leader's language. He'll refer to people as "resources"—as if people were interchangeable parts sitting on a machinery shelf. He'll stress the importance of *resource* planning to manage the budget and schedule. He'll plead with his bosses for more *resources* to enlarge the capacity of his department. The leader is the machinist, and his resources are his machine parts.

How You Treat People Determines the Results You Get

A single-minded focus on results often leads directly to treating people poorly. The drive to achieve results becomes the leader's excuse for toughness, saying things like, "Sure, I'm tough. We're under relentless pressure from our competitors, and margins are tight. Being tough creates urgency and motivates people to work hard. My boss is tough on me, so why shouldn't I be tough on the people who work for me?"

To be sure, results matter. But people achieve those results, and when you treat people poorly you'll get poor results. Which brings us back to the central question that people want to ask you: *Do you care about me?* The answer shows up in your treatment of people. You may say that you care about people, but if you never smile, constantly move up deadlines, rarely ask for their opinions or use their input, take credit for their good work, set unrealistic goals, and don't say "thank you" for their hard work, then you don't really care about them. And they know it.

So what does caring look like? When you care about people, you take an interest in their career aspirations. You seek, and value, their opinions. You appreciate that each person has a life outside of work that impacts how he or she performs inside of work. You know that people aren't just "resources"; they are the coach of the local soccer club, lay minister at the church, active alumna at the state college, recently widowed husband to a wife who died after a long battle with breast cancer, and father to three heartbroken kids.

Answering "yes" to the core *do-you-care-about-me* question means taking a deep and genuine interest in those you are leading. Caring, in this sense, is obliging. For when you care about people, you give them more of your time, attention, and active support. A wise leader treats people as more important than results, because strong people produce those results. Period.

CARING BEGETS CARING

As a practical matter, it's a good idea to care about your people. Here's why: when they know you care about them, they will care about you ... and your success. In fact, you'll know that you're truly a leader who cares when the people you lead start seeking and valuing *your* input, when they take an interest in *your* career aspirations, and when they are actively supportive of *you*. And when your people care about you, they'll help you get better results.

Much of this book is about the metaphorical doors that open-door leaders open for the people they lead. But there's one more door that you have to open before you can fully call yourself an open-door leader: the door to your heart. The people you lead need to see that behind whatever shell you portray lives an imperfect being just like them. They need to know that, despite whatever successes you've achieved, whatever power you've amassed, and whatever perks you get, you're still "real." They want to know that however big your britches are, you still have a sympathetic heart that they will always be able to reach. As long as people know that you have a good and open heart, they will let you push them, give them tough feedback, and ask them to do more. Power works best when it's anchored in humility.

HEAD SMOOSHING TO SHOW YOU CARE

Some people just aren't the feeling type. That doesn't mean they don't care. They just don't show their caring through their emotions. My son Ian, for example, is not a touchy-feely little tyke. To the contrary, he's a rough-'n'-tumble boy, often with mud on his face and dirt on his feet. He tends to shy away from sentimental stuff. One day, for example, Ian was jumping on our backyard trampoline with Alex and Bina, his brother and sister. I called down from our back deck to let them know I was going away on a business trip, telling them, "I love you, kids!" Bina responded, "I love you too, Daddy!" Then Alex chimed in, "I love you too, Daddy!" Then Ian replied, "I love your shirt, Dad!"

Like many people, Ian is uncomfortable showing his emotions, and that's perfectly fine. Unlike his brother and sister, Ian has never been one to come up and spontaneously kiss me on the cheek. However, sometimes he does slap both of my cheeks, pull my face toward his, grit his teeth, and smoosh his forehead into mine as hard as he can. I consider it his way of showing me that he cares.

The important thing is to show your caring heart in whatever way you can. Just check with HR before smooshing somebody's head.

SHOWING THAT YOU CARE

Showing how much you care doesn't come easy for some leaders, especially the more introverted or analytical types. Keep it simple, and let your actions speak louder than your mouth. Don't just tell people you care about them; show them! Here are some real-life examples:

- The owner of a Chicago-based highway construction business makes it a point to visit his night crews during the largest and worst snowstorms. Having come up through the ranks, he knows that your crews respect you more when you show you care about them, especially when it would be more convenient not to.
- A partner at a law firm regularly takes starting lawyers out to lunch. But instead of taking them to the fancy restaurant downtown where other law firms dine, he takes them to the down-home barbeque place by the railroad tracks next to a prison. Why? It loosens people up—you literally have to drape your necktie over your shoulder so it doesn't fall into the sloppy food! The informal lunches help the partner get to know his people in an informal way.

- The CIO of a large office management company catches people off guard by beginning the annual strategic-planning meeting in an unexpected way. He stands in front of the twelve executives, looks each person in the eyes, and tells each person why he is grateful that he or she is a member of his team. As a painfully introverted technologist, being this socially vulnerable is extremely uncomfortable. But he does it anyway. As he goes on, both he and his team well up with emotion. It's clear that he cares about them, deeply.
- The owner of a successful event management company takes her staff on a yearly "sanity" outing. Each outing is held at a different resort, and the choice of resort is based on the quality of its spa. She makes sure her team is thoroughly and luxuriously pampered. Managing large-scale events is insanely demanding, and taking care of her staff ensures that they will take care of her business (and customers).

TOUGH LIKE AN M&M

Dick wasn't some touchy-feely, bleeding-heart organizational-development wimp. He also wasn't the type of person who wore his emotions on his sleeve. So it was hard to know whether he cared about me, or whether I should care about him.

After hanging up my Speedo and retiring from the US High Diving Team, I got my first "real" job. I worked for High Performing Systems, a leadership-development consulting firm based in Athens, Georgia. My boss, Dick Thompson, was a no-nonsense ex-military officer who had done two tours in Vietnam and had been decorated for heroism multiple times as a member of the elite Green Berets. While I greatly admired Dick, I was very intimidated by him. He was tough, quiet, and intense. He walked with an iron-rod posture, talked in a concise and clipped manner, and could stare right through you when he was upset. Dick was a Southern Baptist who held a black belt in karate. I worked for a boss who could literally kill me with his bare hands if he wanted to and believed that God would be on his side if he did.

One day Dick and I set out on a two-hour drive up to the mountains of North Georgia. We were setting out to lead a three-day adventure-based leadership-development program with an international forest resource company. Dick and I would be cofacilitating, and much of the training event would be spent wearing army fatigues. I was thrilled at the prospect of working side by side with someone who knew so much about leadership—not just from textbooks (Dick had a PhD in psychology) but from years spent in the trenches leading teams in do-or-die situations. Though I was thrilled, it still bugged me that I didn't have any sense of who Dick was behind his rigid exterior.

Then Dick did something that helped me see him in a totally different light. As he turned the ignition key, he turned to me and said, "Would you mind if I put on a little music for the drive?" Thinking that I was about to get a two-hour dose of old-timey gospel music, I answered unenthusiastically, "Fine with me." Then, out of the car speakers, to my pleasant surprise, came the screeching guitar notes of Creedence Clearwater Revival's famous Vietnam War song "Run through the Jungle." With that, Dick hit the gas pedal, leaving a small patch of rubber on the pavement.

For the next two hours, with John Fogerty singing in the background, Dick and I talked about his days in the battlefield fighting the Viet Cong. He opened up to me, sharing stories about what it was like to be a member of the Special Forces. I learned that he had spent much of his time in covert operations behind enemy lines. He talked about what leadership meant to him and how his Vietnam experience had influenced and shaped his ideas about leadership. He talked about what it felt like to be responsible for people's lives, not in some abstract way, but literally. He talked about the strong bonds that would form when Dick and his teammates faced firefights together, and how the pain would linger for weeks after a teammate was killed. The more we talked, the more open Dick got, and the more he revealed to me, the more I appreciated Dick as a human being and not just as my boss.

Dick Thompson was like many proud leaders. Like an M&M candy, they're hard and crusty on the outside but sweet and softer on the inside. Sure, he was intense and a little hard to get to know, but once you got to know him better, you learned that he was honest, decent, and good at the core. Most people are. It just takes getting to know them to see their inherent goodness. Dick wasn't just my boss; he was a human being who had had some hard and amazing life experiences. He was someone I could admire, learn from, and listen to rock 'n' roll with.

OPENING YOURSELF

When relationships become more personal, more caring usually results. That caring comes with a risk for a leader. When you care about people, you become more sensitive to their needs. Their interests and opinions become harder to dismiss or ignore. Real relationship is obliging. The fear some leaders have is that in caring for others, they'll lose objectivity or independence and be taken advantage of in the process. While these risks exist, the greater danger is in being remote, aloof, and rigid with the people you lead. When you're as accessible as a stone obelisk, your people will secretly wish for your failure. Conversely, when people care about you as a leader, they'll strive harder to help you succeed. Regardless of whatever reservations you may have, you can't be an open-door leader without opening up to your people. Below are a few simple starting points. Others are provided in the *Actions and Reflections* section.

- Get out of your office. Don't cloister. Walk the halls.

Dedicate a few hours each day to not looking at a screen of any sort.

- Smile more. People won't approach you if you're a perpetual grump.
- Set up and post a LinkedIn profile so people can view your educational background and career history if they want to.
- Display a few pictures from your outside-of-work life and/or your family.
- If your company sponsors a softball league (etc.) or folks get together for trivia night (etc.), join in the fun. Participating in casual activities should help defrost you.
- Use these words liberally and sincerely: "Thank you."

Do these things even if you're uncomfortable. Strike that. Do them *especially* if you're uncomfortable. Remember that doing uncomfortable things is how you grow.

OPEN-DOOR ACTIONS AND REFLECTIONS:

- Reflect on the core question *"Do you care about me?"* Do you think your boss does or doesn't care about you? Why?
- Now think about the people working for you: Do you honestly care about them? How do you think they would answer that question? What evidence would they provide?
- Are there some employees that you care about more than others? Why? What would have to happen for you to take a greater interest in the people you care about the least?
- Think of a leader with whom you've worked who was hard to get to know at first. What happened

that eventually helped you see the leader differently? Before getting to know him or her, did you think the leader cared about you? How about after getting to know them?

- How much of your nonwork identity do you reveal to the people you lead? What might the benefits of being more open with them be? What would it take for you to let them see the "real" you?

- Put yourself, and later your team, through a personality survey like the MBTI or DiSC profile. Understand what makes you tick … and what ticks you off.

- Have a "Bring an Object to Work Day." Have each team member, including yourself, bring an object from home that best reflects "what you're all about."

- Start checking in *with* people, not *on* them. Ask, "How are you doing?" not "How is the project coming along?" Show them that you care about them beyond what they're getting done for you.

CONCLUSION

LEADING DOOR TO DOOR

The arc of open-door leadership is extended when the people you've opened doors for start opening doors for others. The sweetest reward is having a door opened for you by someone who's become a leader with your help.

One of my favorite career moments happened twenty years after I worked with Dick Thompson, the Vietnam vet whom I spoke about in the last chapter. Through the encouragement and support of open-door leaders like Dick, I had started my own leadership-development company—Giant Leap Consulting. One of my clients wanted to conduct a workshop on how to lead during stressful times. Guess who I called? Yep, Dick Thompson.

Two decades after learning about leadership from Dick, I hired him to conduct a stress-management workshop for a group of leaders I was leading. I opened a door for a guy who had opened so many doors for me. And why not? I knew him well and had confidence in the job he'd do. He was suited for the opportunity (having done two stressful tours in Vietnam and having authored *The Stress Effect* [Jossey Bass, 2010]). I had a clear picture of how thrilled the participants would be to hear from a true hero. And I looked forward to giving him all the support he needed to be successful.

My favorite part of this moment was being able to honor Dick

Thompson by introducing him to the group, telling Dick and everyone else in the room how much I cared about him and how grateful I was to have learned from someone who genuinely cared about me. I was both a better professional and human being for having worked with Dick Thompson.

The legacy of open-door leadership is more open-door leadership. When leaders open doors of opportunity for others, they can make a lasting impact on other people who can then open new doors of opportunity for others. Leadership, then, isn't some complex and abstract concept. It is simply a tradition. Leadership is a set of practices and ideals that we pass from one person to another, across organizations and generations. It is a tradition that makes people's lives better by creating opportunities for them to thrive, achieve, and lead. We share in the rich tradition of leadership when all of our efforts stay directed on one thing: continually opening doors for each other.

A FINAL ACTION:

- Taking into account all you've read about open-door leadership, what specific actions will you take to be an open-door leader? Write your answer below and hold your feet to the fire with a timeline:

Acknowledgments

Countless doors were opened for me during the writing of this book. I am especially grateful to the many author and client friends who took the time to review early drafts of the manuscript and gave me invaluable improvement suggestions. Especially useful feedback came from Chip Bell, BJ Gallagher, Sharon Jordan-Evans, Mark Levy, Maren Showkeir, Charles Lang, and Naomi George.

Nancy Breuer served as my Virgil as I navigated through the writing of this book. She mentored, educated, and cajoled me into writing a better book than I first shared with her. She's a wonderful editor with whom to share a book journey. The editors at iUniverse and Open Book Editions (a division of Berrett-Koehler Publishers) offered great editorial input as well.

I continue to be indebted to my wonderful clients. They've provided me with a meaningful and fulfilling career. I am always grateful when clients become true friends. I hesitate to name specific people for fear of excluding or forgetting people. Some people do, however, deserve special recognition; namely, Mike Calihan, Craig Atkinson, Steve Rivi, Sandra Alexander, Gail Tolbert, Naomi George, Thomas Schwerzmann, Marie Guevara, Tina Meyer, and Lynn Morgan.

Giant Leap Consulting was founded over a decade ago. The company would have gone off the rails years ago were it not for the wonderful courage, commitment, and ownership of current and former Giant Leapers, including Laura Cohn, Becky Jarrell, Ahli Moore, Michelle Sissine, Charles Lang, and Brooke Weston.

I love my children. They love me. What more can a parent ask for? Being a father to Alex, Bina, and Ian has made me a richer and better person. Much of what I do, I do because of my love for them. I love you, kids! I am proud of you!

Having written is easier than writing. Writers, including me, can be a little moody during the writing process. I think my wife would agree, though, that this book put me in a better and lighter mood than my previous books did. Thankfully my wife has become quite experienced at living with me when I'm in "writer mode." I love you, Shannon.

Finally, I would like to thank all the dead people! I am a spiritual guy, and I am grateful to those friends and loved ones who have traveled beyond life's veil. I am especially grateful to my grandmother GooGoo. I grew up a lower-middle-class kid in an upper-class town. GooGoo always taught me to hold my chin up high. Thanks, GooGoo, for blessing me with your Irish, Nordic, Celtic spirit!

About the Author

Bill Treasurer is the founder and chief encouragement officer at Giant Leap Consulting (GLC), a company that exists to help people and organizations live more courageously. He is widely regarded as the originator of the new organizational-development practice of courage building.

Bill is the author of the internationally best-selling book *Courage Goes to Work*. The book provides practical strategies for inspiring more courageous behavior in workplace settings.

He is also the creator of a do-it-yourself leadership-training program, *Courageous Leadership: Using Courage to Transform the Workplace*. The program promotes managerial courage and has been taught to thousands of executives throughout the world. Learn more at www.pfeiffer.com/go/courage.

Since 1991 Bill has led over five hundred corporate workshops and webinars for notable clients, such as NASA, Saks Fifth Avenue, Accenture, Monster.com, Bank of America, CNN, Spanx, the Center for Creative Leadership, Hugo Boss, UBS Bank, PNC Bank, the US Forest Service, the National Science Foundation, and the US Department of Veterans Affairs. Learn more at www.couragebuilding.com.

Bill's insights have been featured in more than one hundred newspapers, including the *Washington Post*, the *New York Daily News*, the *Chicago Tribune*, the *Atlanta Journal Constitution*, the

Boston Herald, and *Investor's Business Daily*. Bill's insights have also appeared in such magazines as *Leader to Leader*, *Leadership Excellence*, *Business-to-Business*, *Parents Magazine*, *Redbook*, *Women's Day*, *Training Magazine*, and the *Harvard Management Update*.

Prior to founding Giant Leap Consulting, Bill was an executive in the change management and human performance practice at Accenture, a twenty-five-billion-dollar management consulting firm. Bill became Accenture's first full-time internal executive coach and coached Accenture senior executives to become more courageous leaders.

Bill's first book, *Right Risk*, is about how to take smart risks. Bill is a former captain of the US High Diving Team. For seven years, he traveled throughout the world performing with a team of high-performing athletes. During that time, Bill did more than 1,500 high dives from heights that scaled to over one hundred feet … sometimes on fire!

Bill holds a master of science degree from the University of Wisconsin and graduated from West Virginia University on a full athletic scholarship. He serves as board chairman for Leadership Asheville, is on the board of his local YMCA, and fights for the rights of people with disabilities, including his daughter, Bina.

Contact Bill at: btreasurer@giantleapconsulting.com

Follow Bill at:
- Twitter: @btreasurer
- LinkedIn: www.linkedin.com/in/courage/
- Facebook: http://facebook.com/bill.treasurer

About Giant Leap Consulting, Inc.

Giant Leap Consulting is a courage-building company on a mission to help people and organizations act with more courage. Since its founding in 2002, Giant Leap Consulting has conducted more than five hundred separate client engagements related to elevating individual employee and organizational performance.

We believe that people work more effectively and with higher levels of passion and commitment when they are operating out of confidence and courage than out of fear and anxiety. Our client engagements are built upon the foundational conviction that people achieve extraordinary results when they engage courageously with one another. In short, our aim is to create *courageous organizations.*

Giant Leap's four service lines are:

- **Courageous Future:** Strategic-planning services designed to help organizations create a bold and compelling future

- **Courageous Leadership:** Leadership and succession-planning programs and curricula designed to create courageous leaders
- **Courageous Teaming:** High-impact team-building programs that promote honest, responsible, and adult-like behavior from all team members
- **Courageous Development:** Customized training programs that build individual skills and organizational capabilities. Among others, our training programs include: Courageous Leadership, Culture Change, Conflict Optimization, Motivating Self and Others, Change Leadership, Powerful Presentations, Communication Effectiveness, and Coaching for Peak Performance.

Giant Leap works with profit and nonprofit organizations that aim at a higher standard of performance, including Accenture, PNC Bank, Walsh Construction, Saks Fifth Avenue, Hugo Boss, UBS Bank, Aldridge Electric Incorporated, UNICEF, and many others.

Giant Leap Consulting works extensively with the US government and has worked with the Centers for Disease Control and Prevention (CDC), the National Science Foundation, the US Department of Veterans Affairs, the US Army, the US Forest Service, and NASA. We are proud to be a GSA-approved provider.

To learn more, please visit our websites: giantleapconsulting.com, couragebuilding.com, managerialcourage.com, and www.pfeiffer.com/go/courage.

Follow Giant Leap Consulting at:
- Twitter: @takegiantleaps
- LinkedIn: www.linkedin.com/in/courage/
- "Like" us on Facebook! (search for Giant Leap Consulting)

OPEN BOOK EDITIONS
A Berrett-Koehler Partner

Open Book Editions is a joint venture between Berrett-Koehler Publishers and Author Solutions, the market leader in self-publishing. There are many more aspiring authors who share Berrett-Koehler's mission than we can sustainably publish. To serve these authors, Open Book Editions offers a comprehensive self-publishing opportunity.

A SHARED MISSION

Open Book Editions welcomes authors who share the Berrett-Koehler mission—Creating a World That Works for All. We believe that to truly create a better world, action is needed at all levels—individual, organizational, and societal. At the individual level, our publications help people align their lives with their values and with their aspirations for a better world. At the organizational level, we promote progressive leadership and management practices, socially responsible approaches to business, and humane and effective organizations. At the societal level, we publish content that advances social and economic justice, shared prosperity, sustainability, and new solutions to national and global issues.

Open Book Editions represents a new way to further the BK mission and expand our community. We look forward to helping more authors challenge conventional thinking, introduce new ideas, and foster positive change.

For more information, see the Open Book Editions website:
http://www.iuniverse.com/Packages/OpenBookEditions.aspx

Join the BK Community! See exclusive author videos, join discussion groups, find out about upcoming events, read author blogs, and much more!
http://bkcommunity.com/

CPSIA information can be obtained at www.ICGtesting.com
Printed in the USA
BVOW072359230513

321530BV00002B/23/P